the GOOD NEWS *about* WORRY

Books by
Dr. William Backus

The Good News About Worry

The Healing Power of a Christian Mind

Learning to Tell Myself the Truth

Telling Each Other the Truth

Telling the Truth to Troubled People

Telling Yourself the Truth (with Marie Chapian)

What Your Counselor Never Told You

Applying Biblical Truth to Problems
of Anxiety and Fear

the

GOOD
NEWS

about

WORRY

Dr. William Backus

BETHANYHOUSE
MINNEAPOLIS, MINNESOTA

Published by Bethany House Publishers
11400 Hampshire Avenue South
Minneapolis, Minnesota 55438

Bethany House Publishers is a division of
Baker Publishing Group, Grand Rapids, Michigan

Printed in the United States of America

In keeping with biblical principles of
creation stewardship, Baker Publishing Group advocates the responsible
use of our natural resources. As a
member of the Green Press Initiative,
our company uses recycled paper
when possible. The text paper of
this book is comprised of 30% post-
consumer waste.

**green
press**
INITIATIVE

Library of Congress Cataloging-in-Publication Data

Backus, William D.
    The good news about worry : applying biblical truth to problems of anxiety and fear / Wil-
liam Backus.
        p   cm.
    Includes bibliographical references and index.
    Summary: "A Christian psychologist explains how to ease and reduce anxiety by replacing
worry-producing thoughts"—Provided by publisher.
    ISBN 978-1-55661-187-2 (pbk. : alk. paper) 1. Anxiety 2. Worry. 3. Anxiety—Religious
aspects—Christianity. 4. Worry—Religious aspects—Christianity. I. Title.
    BF575.A6B23   2010
    248.8'6—dc22

                                                                            2010006253

To Jeff, Judi, Kevin, and Mark

CONTENTS

INTRODUCTION

Who wouldn't want help with anxiety? On at least a few occasions in life, nearly everyone would gladly swallow a potent anxiolytic (medicine for anxiety). Few of us relish the sweating palms, the gnawing in the pit of the stomach (sanguinely called "butterflies" by some), the weak knees, the dry mouth, and the pounding heart that often accompany worry and anxiety. And none relish the dark hours of nocturnal tossing and turning until one's pillow is wadded into a lump and one's bedclothes are knotted and tangled.

But no drug will rid our lives of anxiety, no psychotherapy can take it all away, and no religion will cause it to vanish like the morning dew. Anxiety remains part of life. You have it because you are a human being existing between time and eternity, surrounded from cradle to grave with what the ancient prayer describes as "so many and so great dangers."

So what's my book supposed to do for you if nothing will remove anxiety from our lives?

It's true, the good news about anxiety is *not* that anxiety won't exist after you read this book. The good news about anxiety is that there is a way to deal with it in faith, so as to make the most of it, diminish its power, and find your way through it. If you are willing to stop adding to the problem by seeking every which way to escape and avoid anxiety, if you are willing to let your faith become activated and to follow it straight ahead into your fear, you can discover how to ease and reduce anxiety, and even use it to become the person God wants you to be.

The approach I'm taking may seem strange to you—even questionable. In essence, it's this: Instead of running away from anxiety, step firmly *into* it. Although this notion may sound peculiar, it's very, very old. And it works. It works to give us courage, it works to exercise our faith, and it works to reduce (not eliminate) anxiety from our lives.

I have included a number of examples from the lives of real people. A few of them are friends and relatives, and in several such instances there is no effort to disguise them. But when material from my clinical practice is used, the cases are homogenized, disguised, and made unrecognizable for the very good reason that all clients must be assured absolute confidentiality. However, the purported facts are true. They are not imagined, nor are they wishful thinking. They happened. It's just that you can't tell from reading the material to whom they happened.

Does Everybody Get Anxious?

Lee and I met at the refreshment table during a church coffee hour. As often happens when people find out I'm a clinical psychologist, the conversation soon turned to common human problems and their psychological and spiritual implications. Before long, this young man was sharing his worries with me.

"I can't seem to make my paycheck stretch—*ever*—to pay all the bills," Lee said. "I don't want Sandy to work outside our home because Jill and Ethan need their mother, so we're trying to get by on what I make as a shoe store manager. But there's never enough."

According to Lee, about the time he thinks he can see the way to get through the month, something unexpected comes up: Jill needs orthodontic work; Ethan needs winter clothes; Sandy's allergies flare up. One visit to the doctor and the resulting prescriptions can devour a hundred dollars, and then they're buried in unpaid bills again.

The result? Lee loses sleep for about half of each pay period, wondering what to do until the next paycheck. Worse yet, Lee is concerned about the fact that he worries when he ought to be trusting God.

"I try," he said, "but somehow I get through praying, and an hour later I'm fighting my anxiety again—this sense that the bottom is going to fall out. And I know it's wrong!" Lee believes he's not the kind of Christian he ought to be as long as he worries in this way, so he's miserable. When he grows anxious, he feels wrong for not trusting God. He wants to break the cycle and have the peace of God that "transcends all understanding" the Bible talks about (Philippians 4:6–7).

Lee was reaching out for help. But I had no more expertise than he had in managing money; in fact, I could remember the earliest years of my own marriage, with busted budgets, skimpy clothing allowances, and a steady diet of hamburger. Instead of financial advice, I tried to make some suggestions about how to cut back on his worries.

It's Not the Same for Everyone

Lee is not alone. Everybody experiences anxiety to some degree or another. In fact, anxiety is a condition of mind that lurks behind much of our thinking. It conditions our response to life in countless ways, often limiting us and limiting what God can do through us.

Of course, not everybody gets anxious in the same way or for the same reasons. For some, anxiety is slight, and so it's normally ignored. For others, anxiety is so massive the sufferer nearly stops functioning. Some anxious people appear cool and collected, while others can't seem to hide their jitters from the world.

Imagine, if you will, three different people in Lee's financial bind. The first might be an "avoider." Though he feels a rush of panic on becoming aware of another financial shortfall, he simply sits and watches late-night TV, avoiding the entire mess until he starts receiving threatening letters from creditors.

A second person in the same situation might pay immediately, even reducing his standard of living to meet his obligations. Yet he is miserable, tightfisted, envious of those who have something he doesn't have, and resentful toward God. He also fears constantly that future needs won't be met.

A third person might become emotionally paralyzed. He's not about to make any budget changes, look for a new job, or indeed do anything to solve his problems. To him, any move could turn peril into outright disaster. So he "freeze-frames" his life, stopped in his track by the fear of what awful things might come to pass as a result of his financial difficulties.

Of course, finances are just one potential source of anxiety. Most people experience some anxiety when they have to make a speech or perform in public. Our physical health can be another subject of worry.

I remember, for example, one jewel-like morning in late spring. I got up at five o'clock. The western sky was still dark and the eastern horizon was only beginning to lighten. Ready for a beautiful day, I raced outside, and bent over to turn on the pump for lifting the snow melt off the cover of our backyard pool.

Suddenly I felt something warm spurting from my nose, and red drops splashed on the concrete. A nosebleed? Me? I hadn't had a nosebleed since—well, I couldn't even remember when. I wasn't worried, but I was puzzled.

Walking back inside, I sat down and waited for the bleeding to stop. Surely it would be only a matter of minutes! Yet the time dragged on, and the bleeding continued.

Seven hours and two hospital emergency rooms later, I half-jokingly asked the specialist examining me whether it's possible to die from a nosebleed. He frowned, said yes, and with special instruments probed a spurting artery high in my left nostril. Then he cauterized the blood vessel.

At last the bleeding stopped. I had lost several pints of blood, and for weeks I could hardly move without exhaustion.

One night about two weeks later, I awoke at 2 A.M. Was I dreaming or really feeling warm wetness running from my left nostril? Not another nosebleed! Where would I get help in the middle of the night?

Hoping against hope, though the technique had failed before, I pinched my nostrils together and held them tightly for fifteen minutes. Then, apprehensively, I let go. The bleeding had stopped.

But now I was afraid to move. Would the trouble start again? Would it last again for seven hours? How much more hemoglobin could I afford to lose? I still hadn't recovered from the debilitating effects of the last hemorrhage, and now this?

At last, moving gingerly, I crawled back into bed. Should I move my head? Would I somehow jar open an artery? Could I turn over? Better not.

Meanwhile, I felt the anxiety. Everywhere. My muscles were tense. My heart pounded. My eyes would hardly close. My breathing was shallow. I didn't move for the entire night, and it was a long time before the anxious panic gradually subsided and I fell asleep.

Types of Anxiety

People not only differ in the way they react to worry and anxiety, they experience several kinds of anxiety that afflict them differently.

First is the kind of anxiety that comes on seemingly out of the blue. It blindsides people: Fear, suddenly and without warning, overwhelms them.

"I was sitting in the school auditorium watching my daughter's class program," said a new client during his first visit to my office. "All of a sudden, it hit me! I thought I was dying. I couldn't breathe, my heart was racing. I felt dizzy, hot, weak."

This man thought he was having a heart attack. He had to lie down while his wife called the medics. The doctors at the hospital ran tests, but concluded it was "just anxiety."

This client had no idea what was happening, and even less awareness of the source of his internal earthquakes. So the sudden anxiety tidal wave quickly created a second wave of fear: fear of the fear itself. Many like him, who have experienced one such episode, bend their lives out of shape trying to forestall subsequent attacks.

A second kind of anxiety is perhaps even more common than the first. People experience this anxiety as a chronic vague awareness of fear, a tiny uncomfortable shock in the solar plexus. Many become accustomed to this discomfort, and eventually ignore the fearful thoughts and images lurking around the edge of their awareness.

A third kind of anxiety occurs within people who feel completely comfortable most of the time, and who maintain their feelings of well-being rather easily, for the object of their fear is circumscribed and easy to stay away from. For example, if they faint at the sight of blood, they can nearly always avoid watching people bleed by never going to see a violent movie and driving on when they encounter an accident. They can even shut their eyes or turn their head to avoid looking at blood.

A fourth kind of anxiety totally takes over the lives of some people. It grows and multiplies to the point where they fear nearly everything. They won't leave their homes to go to the store, the doctor, or even the home of their best friend.

Still another kind of anxiety happens to people who are plagued by recurring images or "inner voices" crying doom—what some psychologists have called negative *self-talk.* Their misery is caused by an ongoing monologue in the mind, warning them of what *might* happen, and perhaps of precautions they ought to take to prevent the catastrophes with which they seem threatened on every hand. *What if I get stuck with some boring person at the party and can't get away?* they might think. *Maybe I shouldn't go.*

Predicting dire results comes naturally to these people. For instance: "What if this pain in my side is cancer?" "The boss cut me off when I tried to make a suggestion. Maybe she doesn't like the job I'm doing. What if I get fired?" To use an old phrase, they "borrow trouble."

What Makes People Anxious?

Sometimes we don't know why we have the jitters. The nervousness just comes on for no apparent reason. But at other times we know exactly what we're afraid of when we're anxious. We may have a test to take, for instance, or a salary review coming up. There appears to be no end of the things we can fear and get anxious about.

Here's a brief list of some things people most commonly worry about. You've probably feared some of these things yourself at one time or another:

- someone's disagreement, disapproval, or censure
- loss of love
- being evaluated
- physical injury or illness
- performing for others
- dying
- pain, distress, discomfort
- loss of control
- threats to a child's health or happiness
- change, the unknown

For some people, sudden panic can be provoked by one or more of these situations:

- being locked in a small closed room
- having to talk with a group of strangers
- riding a horse
- standing on a high balcony looking down
- telling someone you're displeased with him
- using a public restroom
- being alone in a dark room
- being in the same room with a dog (even a puppy)
- flying in an airplane

For still others, chronic, somewhat debilitating anxieties can interfere with living to a greater or lesser extent. Some people habitually fear situations or possibilities like these:

- failure
- intimacy
- openness to others
- change in anything—job, residence, friends, routine
- poverty
- sexual performance
- germs on anything
- being judged by God

These lists include only a sampling to give an idea how common anxiety can be in our lives.

What is Anxiety, Anyway?

Sometimes people identify distress in their lives as anger or depression when in reality it's anxiety. They don't recognize it as anxiety because they don't understand anxiety very well. What is anxiety?

Anxiety is fear that we'll be hurt, made to suffer pain, loss, embarrassment, harassment, inconveniences, or other things we judge "not good." The bottom line for many is the fear of death—fear that we'll be killed, wiped out, vaporized, rendered non-existent.

Dr. Hans Selye, the great research physiologist, spent his life studying the effects of stress. His description of our physical reaction to threat—which he called the "fight or flight syndrome"—can help us understand the nature of anxiety.[1]

According to Selye, when the brain perceives danger, it sends an electrical alarm to a gland called the hypothalamus, which acts as a switchboard connecting the mind-to-body functioning. This gland releases a chemical substance to alert the pituitary gland. At that point a material called the adrenal cortical hormone (ACTH) is released in the blood.

This potent chemical triggers the adrenal glands, which send out cortisone, epinephrine, norepinephrine, and a whole conglomeration of biochemicals that cause physical effects we can feel: Our esophagus tightens, we pant, our heartbeat steps up, our stomach stops its digestive activities and diverts blood to the muscles, and our whole vascular system contracts so we won't lose too much blood in case of injury. In this way the body prepares to deal with danger by running away or fighting.

When we react physically to stress this way, our healthy, tuned-up body is crying out for action or release. If the object of fear isn't something we can run from or do battle with, and if we don't know what else to do, we may simply suffer instead the discomfort called "anxiety."

This discomfort can be difficult to characterize, but the common profile of anxiety includes a number of traits. Typically, we sense that something is wrong, out of kilter, or even dangerous. We have a feeling of danger, as though we might be attacked, punished, or harmed in some way. We are tense all over, keyed up, but we can't think of anything we can do about it.

We might be over-alert, concentrating on the threatened feelings, but having difficulty keeping our mind on tasks or thinking. We feel short of breath, as if we can't inhale enough air. We just can't get comfortable. We wish we could relax.

We find ourselves expecting trouble. We remain ill at ease. In some kinds of anxiety, our thoughts focus themselves on the discomfort and on what disasters it may portend, while in other kinds, we ruminate about terrible things that might happen. We wonder where God could be keeping himself, and we find it difficult to pray or even think about God's Word.

Where Anxiety Comes From

Where does our anxiety come from? Did we learn to worry from someone else? Were we born tense and nervous? Is it our diet? How did we come to be so afraid of rejection, of other people, of dying, of germs, of dirt, of failure?

The answer to these questions isn't simple. Anxiety has a number of causes, and for most of us, more than one of them may be operative in a complex interactive process that produces problems.

Born anxious. Most likely, no one is exactly "born anxious." But more and more evidence is accumulating that some people are born with a *tendency* to be more reactive—that is, more likely to get into a fight or flight mode—than others. The reactive types remain more likely to get upset throughout life than the less reactive. Such persons will become anxious more readily than those who are born less reactive.

This is not to say, of course, that our genes compel us to suffer from painful anxiety problems. Even if we were born reactive, we can learn to handle it without becoming paralyzed with fear for the rest of our life.

Radical misbelief. Another cause of fear is our own thinking or internal speech. If you have never discovered your *internal monologue*, now is the time to detect it. Just stop reading for a moment and pay attention to the thoughts in your own mind.

What did you find yourself thinking? Perhaps your mind was pondering the subject of the internal monologue itself: "I wonder if I have an internal monologue like the one he's writing about" or "Yes—I've often noticed that my mind keeps up a constant line of chatter."

Did you know the notions, perceptions, judgments, and opinions reflected in that chatter have a direct effect on our feelings and our behavior? And what we tell ourselves in that internal monologue of ours may be the most significant present cause of our worries and anxieties?

How can that be? It happens when we come to believe certain erroneous notions. I call those notions *misbeliefs* because they are *beliefs* that are *amiss* or fallacious and incorrect. They won't hold water when examined in the light of the truth. Consider, for example, these three misbeliefs that often undergird and perpetuate anxiety:

1. I can't expect God to protect me because I haven't been good enough for Him.
2. I couldn't stand it if, while I am giving a talk, some people should appear bored.
3. I can't ask Joanie to go to church with me; she might think I'm too religious and stop liking me.

These examples and many other similar notions rattle around in all our heads from the time we learn to talk.

Misbeliefs of this nature are acquired in various ways. We may learn them by hearing others repeat them, or by imitating the attitudes we see in others. We may even formulate them ourselves, drawing upon our own creative resources to come to mistaken conclusions. But their ultimate source is the father of lies, the devil, and like him they can be most destructive.

However these misbeliefs are acquired, they elicit and fortify most of our everyday irrational anxieties, fears, and worries. We must learn to discover them and replace them with truth if we want to make headway against distressing or debilitating anxieties.

The Effects of Anxiety

Some people have been led to believe it's just terrible if they ever get anxious. They may think they'll die or go crazy if they have another attack of panic, or that they'll surely have a coronary if they let themselves give in to stress or tension.

The truth, however, is that everybody experiences anxiety. We aren't likely to drop dead from anxiety, nor will it give us a case of chronic, severe mental illness. Anxiety, stress, and tension are normal, and a healthy person can handle even severe levels of stress-related distress. In fact, a life without any stress or anxiety would be a life without challenge. It would likely bore us to death!

On the other hand, stress and tension related to anxiety can, if not handled effectively, cause illness. They can also aggravate other physical ailments. Some kinds of hypertension, headaches, muscle aches, and stomach problems may be related to unrelieved stress from anxiety.

Beyond the physical effects of anxiety are spiritual, emotional, and psychological effects as well. Many people suffer these effects without any awareness that their problem is failure to cope with anxiety of one kind or another.

The Most Widespread Consequence of All

More pervasive than most of the other consequences of anxiety is one we are likely to overlook. Yet it may be the most important. Best of all, this is one consequence we can change if we choose, thus gaining the upper hand over anxiety. That consequence is what psychologists call *avoidance*.

Most anxiety causes us to avoid something—whatever it is that makes us feel the distressing sensations or think the worrisome thoughts involved in being anxious. So, for example, if we are terror-stricken at the prospect of making a speech, we'll probably try to avoid having to talk in front of a crowd. If we worry about running out of money, we'll probably either try to avoid thinking about our precarious financial state, or we'll save every penny to avoid ever coming to the point of a shortfall. If the prospect of failing God frightens us, we may refuse to step out and obey Him by serving others.

One fact about avoidance significant for our discussion is the psychological truth that avoidance is counterproductive. Rather than helping the situation, it perpetuates and worsens anxiety. Like many consequences of our behavior, it has the effect of strengthening the behavior that leads to its occurrence.

Anxiety is Simply Human

In chapter 2 we'll take a closer look at this matter of avoidance, and we'll learn how we can make meaningful headway against anxiety by tackling the problem with the resources of our Christian faith. But before we close this chapter, let's take a look at two vexing questions many will be asking.

1. *Does my anxiety mean I'm a poor Christian?*

Unfortunately, some believers have the impression that every Christian who is worth his baptismal water will be fearless and bold at all times. They compare themselves invidiously with the martyrs facing immolation as living torches at Nero's garden parties, or perhaps with Daniel who went undaunted into the lions' den. "And here *I* am," they think, "about to collapse with anxiety at the idea of having to read a verse to a group of people in Bible class!"

If we tend to think that way, we need to ask ourselves how anxious and fearful those heroes themselves might have felt. Yes, their actions defied danger, but many a hero has admitted that all the time he was acting boldly, his heart was melting with dread and anxiety. Even Jesus sweat blood in anticipation of the cross.

For that reason, our anxiety—even intense anxiety—doesn't prove we are shabby, third-rate Christians. It only proves we are human.

2. *Does anxiety mean I'm a spiritual or emotional baby?*

Not at all. Anxiety, even irrational anxiety, doesn't mean we are a spiritual infant or an emotional wreck. True, the spirit that God has given us does not make us timid (see 2 Timothy 1:7), but we're still working on exercising our freedom from the old sinful flesh to which we died in Christ. So we have to practice disobeying that flesh until it becomes a habit.

The flesh, in cooperation with Satan, might try to reduce us permanently to sniveling heaps of quivering fear. But we can learn to talk back to the flesh until we stop giving place to its impulses and desires altogether. Meanwhile, it's not abnormal or weird to experience some of the flesh's influences—including irrational anxiety.

Whenever Jesus called anyone to faith, He summoned that person to take some action, not just to sit comfortably and think beautiful thoughts. Lee, whom we met at the beginning of this chapter, found it necessary to take some action. He consulted a financial counselor who helped him reorganize his way of dealing with the tight squeezes. By taking effective action, Lee reduced his own anxiety.

As you work through the pages that follow, you too will learn to understand your own anxiety better. You'll see how it affects you physically, mentally, emotionally, and most of all, spiritually. You'll learn to locate and isolate the automatic thoughts that, running unbidden through your mind, stir up those unpleasant, anxious feelings and actions. And you'll learn to replace those pain-causing thoughts and beliefs with solid and real facts based on God's own calming words that lead to the life of peace Jesus promised us.

The truth about anxiety is that to get over it, you need to take action. So instead of berating yourself for worries that plague you or anxieties that distress you, set your switches to take action. Let me show you how to apply faith to your fears, until you have fear on the run.

In the following chapter, we will begin by examining one of the most common problems of all—in fact, one of the root problems of anxiety: *avoidance.*

Chapter 2

The Real Culprit: Avoidance

It's fascinating, the number of ways we human beings have come up with for handling anxiety. I've found some who try to distract themselves from their anxious feelings with loud music or by pinching themselves; some who try to calm down by breathing into paper bags, or by reading lists of positive statements as earnestly as they can; some who carry tranquilizers that they never actually take; and some who try reading helpful material. For those who want to read, plenty of books are available. A quick inventory of only one of my bookshelves turned up *eight* volumes on anxiety. Perhaps you've read some of them yourself.

Leslie, one of my clients, had read and tried the suggestions in several such books. "Ever since my husband and I built our new house," she said, "I've felt this dreadful gnawing in the pit of my stomach. I have trouble sleeping; I've lost weight. And I can't seem to snap out of it. What's wrong?"

Leslie thought that maybe if she got a job and got out of the house more, it would help. But it didn't.

Next she decided to try religion. She talked to a pastor, took instructions in the teachings of his denomination, and joined his church. He thought it would help if she learned more about God, and some friends from the church even prayed for her, but nothing changed very much.

Leslie had even tried visiting out-of-town relatives for a week because a friend said it would help to get away. "But it didn't," she said. "Now we're wondering if we'll have to sell our new house. I feel like giving up."

Leslie also tried several different tranquilizing medications. But no matter what she did to reduce her anxiety, she suffered still from a constant, low-level dread that grew worse when she had to be in the new house—especially alone.

Most people like Leslie have experimented with ways of handling worry, nervousness, or anxiety. Many try one thing after another with meager results. We often try, hoping against hope for good results, what psychologists call avoidance techniques.

The peculiar thing about avoidance is that it may work—temporarily. But in the long run, it can actually maintain our fears and even increase them. So we need to look at some of the avoidance "remedies" we try, to see why they may have failed and why avoidance, which appears so promising at first, usually disappoints us in the long run.

Our Favorite Tactic

"I don't want to see anybody from church. I don't want to talk to anybody. I just want to stay away from all of them!" Cal teared up as he told me how he wanted to avoid interactions with members of his church fellowship.

I had suggested he might be getting well enough to make a start. But he insisted: "It's too hard. I just don't think I can go back. I can't handle it when they ask me questions I don't know how to answer. I don't want them asking me how I'm doing or if I'm feeling better! What can I say, anyway? I know they'll disapprove if I tell them I'm not well yet!"

Four months previously, Cal had suffered what he termed a nervous breakdown after he'd shocked others by uncharacteristically exploding in anger during a class discussion. Afterward he'd stayed at home rather than attend meetings or church services. Some people from the church had tried to call on him, but were told he couldn't see them. Although he did allow a few especially close friends to visit occasionally, he had managed to get others to do his tasks at church, and isolated himself almost completely from everyone connected with the fellowship.

Worse yet, Cal had even begun avoiding stores, parks, movies, restaurants, and other public places for fear of meeting someone from church. His anxiety had snowballed. He declared that he couldn't face other members because of what they might think of his failure to recover immediately and completely. According to Cal, the unwritten rules at his church seemed to require everyone to say, "I'm just wonderful, praise the Lord!" whenever others asked, "How are you?"

I understood how his comfort level improved as he increasingly avoided contacts with anything that might prove embarrassing or difficult, staying safely sealed off in the shelter of his living room. But I also realized that, by thoughtlessly opting for easy comfort, Cal was creating a chronic problem for himself. He would eventually become a recluse if he didn't face the situations he was avoiding, even if he found them difficult and anxiety-provoking.

Even more damaging was an effect Cal couldn't detect: His sense of self-worth and personal significance was slowly but surely eroding. Regardless of the increased comfort level afforded by avoiding anxiety, the awareness that he was failing to do the things he ought to do was growing and would soon convince him that he was a dud and a loser, a coward too chicken to face the situations others seemed to face without any fear at all.

Cal's self-isolation, like most of the devices we come up with ourselves for lessening the pain of anxiety, resulted from avoidance. The strategy of avoidance is common among those who, like Cal, are dealing with anxiety, because it appears to be so natural. Intuitively we expect it to work for us. "If I can just avoid this whole business," we think, "the tension and worry will go away."

Not all avoidance behaviors are as extreme as Cal's. Consider some other common instances of avoidance behavior:

- Dena's new next-door neighbor sounds like a lot of fun. They've had coffee together a few times, and already they're planning shopping trips and visits to the park with the kids. But yesterday, the new friend happened to reveal that she thinks church members are the world's worst hypocrites. Now Dena feels she can't tell Ginny she is a Christian for fear Ginny will end their budding relationship. Already, Dena is accepting avoidance as a solution for her feelings of insecure anxiety about Ginny's disapproval.

- Joseph knew he should talk to his thirteen-year-old son Tim about sexual matters. But every time he thought about it, he felt uptight and tongue-tied, so he put it off. Parental avoidance like this is why public schools have the subject in the academic curriculum.

- Elizabeth was sick and tired of trying to keep her house so clean her mother wouldn't find dust on the TV or cobwebs on the hall closet ceiling. But whenever she thought of trying to tell her mother how she felt, the butterflies in her stomach demanded that she scratch the idea. So she continued smiling and avoiding doing what made her anxious. But her rancor grew.

The list of places and activities people avoid may in fact be endless. As a matter of fact, nearly anything you can think of can become an object of fear and consequent avoidance.

We should note especially that anxiety and avoidance are not problems only of people who get clinical treatment for their distress. Those twin "A's" seem to have a place in everyone's life. So to understand this avoidance tactic better, we must look more closely at some categories of things people tend to avoid: situations, people, hard tasks, thoughts of death, negative feelings, and things we ought to do.

Avoiding Situations

Sometimes we handle anxiety by avoiding *situations*. One of my clients named Drew found he grew so anxious that he was painfully uncomfortable at church services. So Drew "solved" his problem by staying home.

Every Sunday, the Jennings family *sans* Dad would dress up and attend worship together. Meantime, though Drew's tension was kept under control, the kids became puzzled and even resentful. Why, they wondered, if going to God's house was good for *them*, was it bad for *Dad*?

Slowly, a barrier grew up within the family. As they entered their teens, one by one, Drew's children rebelled against the inconsistency. They turned away from their early religious training and experimented with drugs and sex. Eventually their parents had no way of talking with their children without encountering sullen rebellion.

Drew's wife blamed him. And as her anger at him smoldered, their relationship deteriorated. Invisible, intangible, but very real, the rifts in this family slowly isolated a father from his wife and children to the eventual detriment of all.

Drew's avoidance may have kept him from experiencing some uncomfortable feelings. But in the process, avoidance damaged others, as it often does, and family relationships suffered.

Surveys show that more Americans fear speaking before a group than anything else, including snakes, heights, financial problems, or even death. Eighty-five percent of the population say they feel uncomfortably anxious about speaking in public. Most people avoid public speaking if they possibly can. Many of these are uptight in any situation where they must try to communicate with others, sometimes even on a one-to-one level. These people try to avoid communication because it makes them anxious.[1]

Dr. Charles Spielberger, a professor at the University of South

Florida, has studied anxiety in college students. His investigations have shown that students who become painfully anxious when they have to take tests in school most often earn low, sometimes failing, grades—even though some are quite intelligent. The low grades are not caused directly by anxiety, but by the fact that test-anxious students avoid studying because any contact with material related to tests generates uncomfortable anxiety. So they avoid anxious discomfort by never cracking a textbook.[2]

Recently, a woman told me she was avoiding medical treatment for her infertility. "What if it fails?" she asked. "Won't my last hope be gone? As long as I don't try the treatment, I can still hope, still feel that I have a chance."

To keep her hope alive, this woman avoided the very best scientific help available for reaching her treasured goal. Surely she was paying a high price for the thin and maladaptive "comfort" she was buying. Many others like her avoid getting help for their problems because they are anxious, fearing that if help should fail, they would be left with no "last resort" and thus proven utterly hopeless.

If we're habitually tempted to avoid situations that make us anxious, we ought to look the consequences of our habit square in the face: If we avoid our problems, we keep them!

For example, does preparing dinner for guests threaten us, so that we never return dinner invitations? Does confronting people frighten us to the point that we do all we can to avoid it? If so, we're used and abused at other people's whims.

Do we worry ourselves sick about money, never daring to invest in anything for fear of losing? Do we avoid the slightest risk like the man in Jesus' parable (see Mathew 25:14–30), so that all we have to look forward to in retirement is a meager investment income? Avoiding some painful situation, though it may temporarily diminish our anxious feelings, can bring other consequences, which, in the long run, extract a terrible price for what we get in return.

Avoiding People

For some people, anxiety and tension elicited by certain other people are so disturbing that they practice *people avoidance*. People-avoiders often so dislike the anxious tension they feel around those who have angered them, they do everything they can to stay away from such people. Some cross the street to avoid meeting an acquaintance simply because social amenities make them anxious. Still others tremble all over at the thought that they might have to encounter someone they know disapproves of them or is angry with them—and they go to elaborate lengths to avoid meeting such people.

Other people-avoiders, uncomfortable in the presence of talkative, genial extroverts, retreat to corners far away from the groups clustered around the life-of-the-party types. Some avoid the bereaved, afraid of saying the wrong thing. Others avoid the handicapped, anxious lest they do something to upset them.

Perhaps such people avoidance grants us a sigh of relief occasionally. But look at the poor bargain we've struck to get that temporary reprieve from anxiety! Do we berate ourselves as weaklings or cowards and despise ourselves for our fear of others? Have we caused others to avoid us because we've made them feel that without even getting to know them we've decided to dislike them? Have we faced the harsh reality that our loneliness results directly from our choosing a few minutes of lowered distress in exchange for the chance to have meaningful relationships with friends?

Avoiding Hard Tasks

Another common avoidance pattern is to shy away from difficult, unrewarding, painful *tasks*, sometimes using another person as our substitute or buffer. We may tell ourselves, "The more unpleasant, distressing, difficult chores I can get out of doing, the happier I'll be!" But that's only the conclusion a child might reach because of the inability to see ultimate consequences.

For example, confronting our hostile adolescent child may terrify us. So we maneuver our spouse into the front lines to do the disagreeable task and take all the guff we are cleverly managing to avoid. We may obtain relief from the anxiety involved in dealing with our child, but that's in the short range. In the long run, we're straining at least two vital relationships: Our mate and our son or daughter both sense at some level that we're ducking out on our part of an important bargain!

For others of us, making telephone calls for information or reservations is something we'd rather not do. Not that we can't do it, nor does fear of the telephone reduce us to a quivering mass of jelly. But for some reason we're uncomfortable with the phone—perhaps due to some low-level anxiety about coping.

When such calls must be made, we hint that our throat is hoarse. Or maybe we insist that we must take care of something else right then, so that our friend or our spouse finally volunteers. Or if we have an office assistant, we pass the task off to him or her.

In these situations, relief in the short range may be somewhat sweet for us. But in the long run we're using someone else to do what's disagreeable to us. We must look ahead and face up to the inevitable consequences to our relationships at work, at home, at play, at church, and among friends when we nudge hard things off ourselves and onto others.

We mustn't be fooled. Just because people say they're willing, we can't conclude they haven't noticed the pattern and don't resent it.

Avoiding Thoughts About Death

Dr. Ernest Becker, in his Pulitzer prize–winning book *The Denial of Death*,[3] argues that much of our ordinary daily activity aims at helping us forget that we are going to die. According to Becker, human beings have devised an infinite number of procedures for avoiding *thoughts about their own mortality.* The result is that we tend to fill our days with diversions, pointless activities, and meaningless chatter.

Death, the threat of nonbeing, generates so much raw anxiety that we defend ourselves heavily against letting thoughts of it enter our minds. The consequences of such wholesale denial required Becker's entire book to spell out. In particular, we should note that hardly anyone in our culture spends much effort and time preparing for death. As a result, most of us pass through one of the most significant of all personal experiences ignorant and unequipped.

Avoiding Negative Feelings

In many instances, the psychological defenses of denial, repression, and projection (and perhaps others as well) can be acts of avoidance in which we refuse to look squarely at our own feelings because of anxiety that they might overwhelm us. For example, a young man named Hans came to see me because he had developed the ability to avoid experiencing one very common emotion: anger. In fact, Hans told me he couldn't recall having been angry in the past twelve years since he had become a Christian. Hans had joined a fellowship where no one was allowed to become angry and where the expression of anger was never condoned, Moreover, he had grown up in a home where anger never surfaced except when his father exploded in one of his rare but very destructive and terrifying rages.

As we explored what appeared to be a nearly incapacitating problem with anxiety, Hans described instance after instance in which others had overlooked him and his needs, failed to live up to his expectations, and done things which resulted in difficulties for him. When I asked Hans how each of these incidents affected him, he replied that he felt very "hurt." So I encouraged him to describe the incidents, his thoughts, and his feelings.

As he did so, Hans' expressions and tone of voice became increasingly exasperated, strident, and annoyed. Though Hans had denied being angry, his anger would have been obvious to most of us. Only slowly did Hans allow himself to face the fact that his anxiety was his fearful reaction to his own rage.

But why had Hans denied his anger? Why do so many other people fail to recognize their anger? Because they want to avoid a threatening emotion. Hans' own anger frightened him because to him, feeling angry meant he was a spiritual dud, a flop as a Christian.

Without noticing his thoughts, Hans had believed and told himself, "I can't be angry. Anger is dangerous to me and to others. Besides, it's wicked to be angry. So I'm not at all angry—just hurt or disappointed or wounded." No doubt Hans derived some temporary consolation from thinking of himself as invariably mild, moderate, temperate, and controlled. But the consequences of his repression had produced painful emotional difficulties.

The feelings we try to avoid don't evaporate merely because we don't like them or don't want them or think they're evil. Unrecognized, they may continue and worsen, producing emotional and even physical difficulties and problems.

Avoiding What We Ought to Do

Avoidance may steal our peace and joy because many of the situations and activities we avoid in the interest of comfort were placed in our lives by God for a purpose. So we end up avoiding *the very things we ought to do*. Examples of this problem abound.

"I know I ought to do it," we may whimper, "but I never seem to get around to it." Frequently, when we neglect what we ought to do, the motive is uncomfortable anxiety. It doesn't have to be massive anxiety; even a flicker of nervousness will paralyze some of us who believe we shouldn't have *any* discomfort in life. Because we feel anxious and uncertain of ourselves or of the outcome of some venture, we avoid the activity we know very well we should do. We may even avoid doing what we very much *want* to do because we aren't willing to put up with uncomfortable anxiety.

The director of a prominent training school for missionaries once told me that such avoidance is one of the greatest hindrances to people going out to serve God on the mission field. "Even when they have a call from God and thorough preparation for the task," he noted, "they hesitate and sometimes avoid their assignments because of fear: fear of not getting married, fear of getting sick, fear of being kidnapped, and fear of experiencing rejection; but most of all, fear of the unknown."

Some people even avoid prayer because of anxiety lest the prayer not be answered. "I was afraid to lay hands on my friend and pray for his healing," my friend Robert confessed sorrowfully, "because I wondered, what if nothing happened? I'd have looked foolish, wouldn't I?"

Another example is reluctance to obey God's command to be reconciled with one another. We may be alienated from our friends or family members because even the thought of going to another person and begging for reconciliation arouses anxiety in us. Such vulnerability scares us. What if the other person puts us down? What if the other says she doesn't want to resume our relationship? We couldn't stand that. So we avoid seeking accord with someone important to us.

Some people find their tax returns so anxiety-arousing they avoid filing until midnight April 15 every year. Perhaps we avoid funerals because it makes us so uncomfortable to have to say something to the bereaved; important church groups and classes because we might have to say something in public; and people in trouble because we might worry about what we can say to help them. In fact, most of the situations we avoid ought not be avoided because what God has called us to be and do in life nearly always moves us toward precisely those places, people, and activities that anxiety pushes us to shun!

Each time we manage to turn away from some scary "ought," we may gain a little (or even a lot of) relief from anxious distress. But when we insist on honoring our fear by avoiding what is right, we also reap a harvest of self-hatred. We see ourselves as gutless cowards, or disobedient failures. In addition comes the unavoidable guilt from such sins of omission (as theologians have named them). This guilt and sense of inadequacy, besides generating their own stock of distressing feelings, have more long-range power to harm us spiritually and psychologically than we may imagine when we're basking in a bit of temporary relief from threatened discomfort.

Avoiding Through Manipulation

Beyond the negative effects on our own emotional and spiritual well-being, avoidance can damage our relationships with others. The chief temptation here is *manipulation*. When we manipulate others it's often in the service of avoidance so we can keep from doing what makes us anxious.

For example, Greg, one of my clients, never quite got around to visiting his great-aunt who lived a few miles away, though he knew he should. It was so hard to know how to talk to her—he always felt unsure of himself around her. He'd never thought of it as anxiety, but that's what he was experiencing at the thought of having to spend a few hours with his elderly aunt.

Greg's wife, Gail, finally stopped reminding him of his duty and began making regular weekly calls on the lonely old woman herself. Though Greg knew he had manipulated Gail by simple passivity, and though he was ashamed of his own failure to carry out his responsibility to his own kin, he continued to let Gail make the visits. In this way Greg succeeded in avoiding the task. But the temporary relief from anxiety never really made up for the detrimental effect on Greg's self-respect resulting from the dim awareness of his own spinelessness.

Another of my clients, Ava, wouldn't go anywhere without her husband, Paul, not even to the grocery store. "I get so nervous and anxious, I can't stand it," she told everyone. As a result, Paul found himself manipulated into being at Ava's beck and call twenty-four hours a day.

Paul would come home from work to take her to the grocery store, the salon, or the doctor's office. In no way could Ava have commanded so much attention and personal service by being normal and healthy. But her anxiety neurosis along with her avoidance habits gave her vast power to manipulate her compliant husband.

The result was costly. Ava spared herself unpleasant anxiety and gained additional control over Paul by her avoidance habits. But she probably caused resentment to bubble inside Paul. She also found that her own sense of worth and competence was crumbling, though she failed to connect that problem to her manipulativeness.

A student who came to be treated for her test anxiety once told me: "All the time I was in high school, I would feel sick to my stomach when I left for school in the morning. Sometimes, I felt so sick my mother would let me stay home. Later, I began to feel nauseated, sometimes to the point of having to vomit, whenever I had to go into any situation in which I wasn't totally sure of myself." This young woman was manipulating her mother for the sake of avoidance. The strategy caused her to see herself as an incompetent failure.

Manipulating others can be a highly developed, finely honed skill. Those who have mastered the art may be so adept at it that the people they manipulate may not even realize what's happening to them. But everyone involved pays a high price in eroded relationships and damaged self-esteem.

Avoidance, the Central Problem

By now, the point should be clear: The most unexamined and unrecognized aspect of the problem of anxiety is the problem of avoidance. It's the underlying strategy in most tactics aimed at ridding ourselves of anxious distress.

It's important to grasp that reality firmly. As we continue, we'll discover that it's our *avoidance* that creates most of the problems associated with anxiety—not the negative feelings that accompany it.

No doubt those who suffer from anxiety complain primarily about their feelings of distress and discomfort, which are sometimes very potent. They usually believe these feelings are the worst aspect of the problem, and practically all the books on anxiety share their assumption. Consequently, attempts to help usually focus on alleviating the discomfort.

Nevertheless, such an approach fails to recognize precisely how avoidance creates far greater problems. In fact, avoidance fosters and increases *the anxiety itself*. So many people fail to grasp an effective way to become free.

Our approach to overcoming anxiety, then, begins with seeing the place of avoidance behavior in our own life and becoming aware of some of the difficulties avoidance has made for us. "What and how am I avoiding?", far from being a side issue, is the major problem when we're trying to cure anxiety disorders. Of course, few of us take kindly to the news that the very things we're doing for relief could be causing and complicating our fears and worries. But it's true.

Even so, we don't have to settle for pain and discomfort. No, indeed! As a matter of fact, facing and eliminating trouble-making avoidance is only the first step to overcoming anxiety. Once anxiety is faced down and not avoided, freedom is only a few steps away.

In the next chapter, we will consider how to begin the process.

The Classic Double Bind

"If only—but why wish for the impossible?" said Grant, a client I had come to know as a world-class worrier.

"If only?" I asked. He had a tendency to drift off into a private turmoil of worries and obsessions.

"Well, I was just thinking that if only I had enough faith I wouldn't worry so much. Being anxious and worrying are the same as unbelief! I wonder sometimes if I really believe in God at all!"

I'd heard the same thought expressed by others. It usually went nowhere except deeper into despair. Christians dealing with anxiety tend to berate themselves for unbelief, giving themselves even more to worry about.

After all, we may reason, shouldn't our Christian faith give us fearlessness in place of anxiety? Didn't Jesus teach us not to be anxious? Didn't He label anxiety a sign of a faith problem (see Matthew 6:25–33)? And didn't the apostle Paul tell Christians to be anxious about nothing (see Philippians 4:6–7)?

If we condemn ourselves this way, however, we don't usually get better. Instead we increase our anxiety by falling into a classic double bind: We worry not only about our problems but also about our seeming lack of faith in worrying about those problems. It's a downward spiral into misery.

Not Condemnation, But Hope

The only way out of this dilemma is to take a look at God's heart toward those who are anxious. Did God intend for His word on anxiety to be a law, a divine pronouncement of failure condemning the anxious Christian? Do those words of Jesus and His great apostle constitute a put-down? Does our anxiety then prove we are a faithless, ungodly wretch for whom there is no hope?

No! On the contrary, the words of Jesus and Paul are good news, not bad news, for worriers. They offer hope and a way out, not condemnation. Consider these other scriptural passages that show us God's heart:

> In him [Christ] and through faith in him we may approach God with freedom and confidence (Ephesians 3:12). Cast all your anxiety on him because he cares for you (1 Peter 5:7). Peace I leave with you; my peace I give you. . . . Do not let your hearts be troubled and do not be afraid (John 14:27). The Lord is faithful to all his promises and loving toward all he has made. The Lord upholds all those who fall and lifts up all who are bowed down (Psalm 145:13–4). For God hath not given us the spirit of fear; but of power, and of love, and of a sound mind (2 Timothy 1:7 KJV).

These and many other promises show us that God's desire is not to weigh us down with anxiety or condemn us for worrying. Instead, He inspires our hope with the knowledge that He cares for us, He is with us, and He himself will lift us up.

The hope we have is this: There is a way to get better. We don't *have* to remain miserable and anxious. Our faith can provide the solution to our anxiety problem, because coming into *real* faith is the beginning of the end for anxiety.

What Is Faith, and What Does It Do?

What exactly is faith and what does it have to do with curing anxiety? Though faith has a supernatural origin because the Holy Spirit, working through the Word of God, creates it in the human heart, nevertheless faith also has a psychological facet. The human mind does the believing.

Faith is the opposite of *unbelief*. A healthy, fully formed, correct faith is the opposite of *misbelief*—that is, an incorrect belief.[1] Christian faith, then, means *believing the truth*.

Often Christians think that anxiety is a problem involving *un*belief. But actually, it's more often the result of *mis*belief. Not what we *fail* to believe, but what we *mistakenly* believe, lies behind much of our worry.

Some of our common notions about faith are not true. For example, an agnostic teacher regularly challenged his Christian students by insisting that if they really had the faith they claimed to have in God's omnipotence, they'd believe God could make a stone so big He wouldn't be able to lift it. His challenge was an empty one because faith is not a matter of forcing ourselves to accept the illogical, the contradictory, or the impossible.

Another example would be my client named Reanna who prayed that God would give her the faith to love her illicit lover so much she wouldn't feel insecure in her adulterous relationship. But faith isn't the ability to believe God will do whatever you want, *regardless* of His stated will.

Faith isn't sheer bravado, bluster, and swagger. Faith isn't presumption. It isn't nonchalantly spending money you don't have for things you happen to want, all the while "believing God for" the necessary finances. It's not exposing yourself carelessly to some dreadful venereal disease, declaring firmly that God will protect you. Nor is faith quitting your job and sitting around waiting for God to provide. Remember,

Jesus himself refused to turn faith into a game of "I double dare you" (see Matthew 4:5–7).

Knowledge, Assent, and Trust

One classical definition of faith is that it consists of *knowledge, assent (or agreement), and trust,* with emphasis on the *trust.*[2] Spelled out, this explanation reveals that we must first *know* some facts: what God says about himself; who Jesus Christ is; what He has done for us; what God, for Christ's sake, can be counted on to do; and who we are in and through Jesus Christ.

But intellectually apprehending these and other truths is not enough. We must give them our *assent,* or agree with them, saying that they are so and meaning it while we stop declaring erroneous beliefs to ourselves. Our self-talk must be made up of right belief, not belief in falsehoods.

Even so, such agreement is not all there is to faith. After knowing the facts and assenting to them, it is crucial that we *trust* Christ Jesus our Savior and God our Father. And we must ordinarily have the first two elements in some measure to arrive at real trust. We must ordinarily *know* something about Jesus and come to the conclusion that the things we know about Him are correct or *true* before it's possible to put *trust* in Him.

This is not to say that God has never worked faith in people who have little knowledge. The blind man in John 9, for example, was ready to believe anything Jesus told him to believe though he evidently didn't know much about who Jesus was. No doubt *trust* is the crucial element in faith, and the extent of our knowledge and agreement may be slight indeed yet generate saving faith. But knowledge, however minimal, is the beginning of faith, because we can't believe or trust what we don't know.

Furthermore, both the Bible and psychological research about how we think concur that if we do know and truly agree that God is who

He says He is, and that Jesus is God himself faithfully carrying out God's promises, we will then come to trust Him. So if there's a lack in our *trust*, it's probably related to a lack in our knowing or agreeing with some significant truth about God or about ourselves. We are most likely not telling ourselves that particular truth in crucial situations, where we need to do so.

The Trust Issue

The focal issue, then, is trust. Many people think of trust as if it were a substance like blood that we have in a certain measure circulating through our system. They believe that having this substance in abundant quantities is what's crucial, and we either have a lot of it or we don't.

But trust is not a substance located inside us. It's really a matter of *action*. Trust is taking action on the basis of something we believe to be so. Trusting the canoe not to spill us into the river means getting into it and taking a ride. Trusting a bank might mean we leave our life's savings at the teller's window and walk away. Trusting our surgeon means climbing up onto the operating table and putting our life in his hands.

On the other hand, if you won't ride in the car with your teenage nephew at the wheel, you obviously don't trust his driving—no matter how much you might *say* you trust him. Our trust is manifested through our behavior.

The German pastor and theologian Dietrich Bonhoeffer pointed out that when Jesus called people to become His disciples, He summoned them to take an action first:

> *The call goes forth, and is at once followed by an act of obedience, not a confession of faith. . . . There is no other road to faith or discipleship—only obedience to the call of Jesus.*[3]

THE GOOD NEWS ABOUT WORRY

This truth is clearly illustrated in the response of Levi and the fishermen Peter, James, and John. Levi, the tax collector, began his faith with an action: "As he [Jesus] walked along, he saw Levi son of Alphaeus sitting at the tax collector's booth. 'Follow me,' Jesus told him, and Levi got up and followed him" (Mark 2:14). To Peter, James, and John, the summons came first to leave their fishing business behind and follow Jesus (see Luke 5:1–11).

When Jesus told Peter to walk out on the water to Him, Peter didn't first receive a short course in the pneumatic physics of specific gravity. Instead, when he was bidden to come, Peter dared to risk his life by stepping out of the boat. And the first step for the rich young ruler was not to take a confirmation class, but to go and sell all and give it away. Only then could he follow Christ.

No doubt, in each case, the disciples experienced anxiety, worry, fear. "What about my business, my income, my investments, my future, my life?" But in each case, faith required *obedient action*.

Notice especially that in each case as well, the action Jesus called them to take was challenging and denied a strategy of *avoidance*. In order to circumvent the action called for, avoidance would have led these people to take care of their own business *first*, find out how to float in case of sinking *first*, and secure their assets *first*. Instead, in each case when someone obeyed the Lord, the action and subsequent events cured the anxiety! And when those like the rich young ruler chose not to obey, they succumbed to anxiety.

True faith, then—the faith which can *cure* because it's a matter of trust based on knowing and agreeing with the truth—consists of *action* commensurate with that truth. Without such action, the apostle James insisted, faith is dead (see James 2). If we trust in Jesus, we believe Him when He says it's good for us to do a particular thing. So we obey His summons and do what He says is good to do, even if it appears unpleasant, painful, or even bad to us.

Having faith thus includes knowing and telling myself that all will be well when I do the will of God. So it's clear that faith includes much more than mere notions about the existence of God. It includes as well our obedience to His will insofar as we know it. In faith, I carry out God's will by doing what is right to do.

Faith: Living, Busy, and Active

Martin Luther learned that faith inevitably spawns responsibility-fulfilling actions:

> *Faith . . . is a divine work in us. . . . O, it is a living, busy, active, mighty thing, this faith; and so it is impossible for us not to do good works incessantly. It does not ask whether there are good works to do, but before the question arises, it has already done them, and is always at the doing of them. He who does not these works is a faith-less man . . . though he talks and talks, with many words, about faith and good works.*[4]

So true faith always includes obedience or *doing your duty*, and it never stops with mere mental activities.

In light of that reality, we can return to the question my client Grant raised. Does our worry and anxiety mean we're not Christians? No! Paradoxically, anxiety can exist right alongside Christian faith within the same believer. Grant's anxiety didn't prove he wasn't a Christian any more than a spoiled spot on an apple proves the rest of the apple isn't edible.

Jesus said: "The spirit is willing, but the flesh is weak" (Matthew 26:41 NASB). The apostle Paul also spoke of the struggle within believers between obeying and resisting God's will (see Romans 7:25). Christians have both flesh and spirit, both sinfulness and righteousness, competing within them to generate their thoughts and behavior.

The spiritual nature—that part of us renewed at rebirth—will inevitably create the true beliefs proper to faith and life. But the old nature tries to drag the renewed person back down into misbeliefs, causing despair, faithlessness, hopelessness, and sin. By sowing its lies and precipitating avoidance rather than obedience, the flesh spawns and maintains anxiety and worries in many of us. If we buy into its efforts to spook us, we end up repeating to ourselves its deceptions.

Anxiety is not in itself a rejection of Jesus' call to duty; that comes with our *disobedience*. So we must target not anxiety but rather *avoidance* behavior where such avoidance means shirking the duty to which we are called by Christ Jesus. Then, as we overcome avoidance, we find that our anxiety is lessened as well, because avoidance keeps anxiety robust.

Avoidance: The Power Source of Anxiety

Hannah was afraid to fly on an airplane, a crippling fear because it usually prevented her from visiting her grandchildren, who were the apple of her eye. She believed the plane would probably crash, and if it did, she would die. Hannah felt fearful just thinking about flying.

Here's how it worked. Anxiety results from believing and telling ourselves untruths, which are the opposite of faith or correct belief. Two core misbeliefs usually give rise to our anxiety.

First, we believe that *something is very likely to turn out badly*, when in all probability it will turn out tolerably well. Second, we believe that *if it does turn out badly, the harm done will be devastating*, when in fact we can recover from even the worst disasters and go on with a life lived in praise of God. As one psychologist put it, the misbeliefs in anxiety involve *over-estimating the probability of a harmful event* and *overestimating the harmfulness of that event*.

In other words, anxiety results from telling myself that God won't protect me and that I can't expect Him to turn bad outcomes into good. In Hannah's case, she was telling herself that a plane crash was much more probable than is the case; it's much less likely than a car crash. In addition, she was telling herself that dying would be terrible, though she hadn't much evidence for that. In fact, dying suddenly in a crash might be one of the easiest ways to get accomplished what we'll all have to go through eventually—and since dying ushers believers into heaven, it's hard to see how it can be the tragic disaster Hannah assumed it was.

In short, then, Hannah was anxious because she *overestimated the probability of a plane crash, and overestimated the harm she would encounter if the crash occurred and she died.*

A good question to ask yourself is how you might be like Hannah. For example, if you tell yourself you couldn't endure it if you lost your job, you're overestimating the awfulness of being laid off or fired. It would be a bad situation, of course, but you could endure it as many people do all the time. The same is true of other possibilities whose harmfulness we tend to overestimate: the loss of health, a financial crisis, problems with our children.

Or consider how we tend to overestimate the probability that a harmful event will occur. For example, if you never go near a Bible class because you might have to read aloud, and you might make a mistake, and if you did other people would certainly think you're stupid, you're betting on some very low probabilities. Reality is otherwise: Many people might not even notice if you made a mistake reading, but the majority of those who did notice would hardly want to bother estimating your IQ. They'd be too busy getting set to read when it's their turn.

Often we overestimate both the likelihood and the intensity of a negative outcome. In the case of the Bible class, you may tell yourself not only that people will probably think you're dumb, but also that it would be awful and intolerable if just one person should think that way. Both of these are misbeliefs. Even if someone *did* think you were stupid, though it might not be the thought you'd most like others to think about you, it's nevertheless not likely to do you much harm either. Why would it be so terrible if someone mistakenly under-estimated the amount of your gray matter?

Notice that here, as in every instance of anxiety, we're saying either that God won't protect us from an almost certain calamity, or that if it does occur, He won't turn it into the highest good. Misbelief, then, is one of the root problems of anxiety. But the other root that causes us so much trouble is the behavior we discussed before: avoidance.

How Avoidance Intensifies Anxiety

One very important fact about anxiety, a fact that must not escape our notice, is that anxiety—like faith—is not entirely a matter of what's in our head. Anxiety also involves behavior, just as faith does. In the case of anxiety, the accompanying behavior is avoidance. That's because anxiety involves some conditioning from past experience as well as belief.

Many of us learned about behavioral conditioning in basic psychology classes. By reading about various conditioning experiments, we found out that a traumatic event may cause any stimuli associated with that event to arouse fear or anxiety in us long after the event is over.

For that reason, anxiety can be more than just a matter of fear generated by misbelief. It can also involve a conditioned response to certain stimuli which have been experienced along with trauma or pain in the past.

Chauntell, for example, was a sophisticated, independent sixteen-year-old who had been driving her car in a snowstorm when another vehicle plowed into her back bumper. Her automobile spun out of control and collided with another car traveling in the opposite direction. Chauntell walked away from the accident, suffering physically from nothing more than some bruised muscles and neck pain. But now Chauntell wouldn't let herself think about driving.

Even when she rode with another driver, Chauntell's heart pounded and her palms perspired. If she let herself think about the collision, she became so uncomfortable she'd switch to thinking of something else. Soon she was avoiding everything that brought on anxiety.

When she came for treatment, it appeared likely to me that most of Chauntell's reaction to her trauma was conditioned autonomic arousal. That is, she was reacting directly to any stimuli associated with the accident without telling herself any particular misbeliefs. So we had to deal with her conditioning rather than misbeliefs.

In a second example, consider a woman named Olivia who recounted her understanding of the way she had developed a fear of the water. The anxiety was so severe, she became terrified even if she contemplated getting into the shallow end of a pool.

"I had these two older brothers," Olivia said, "and they were always tormenting me when I was a little girl. One of the things they did was hold me so I couldn't move and then duck my head under water in our pond. I was terrified because I couldn't breathe! They'd never let me come up until I thought I was going to die!"

Olivia's fear and avoidance are probably conditioned anxiety. Even so, in practice it's difficult to be certain in this and other cases how much of the anxiety is a response to self-talk ("I'm going to drown, I won't be able to breathe, I'll die") and how much to direct conditioning.

In the therapy called *aversive conditioning,* some psychologists believe they are making use of the phenomena of conditioned anxiety and avoidance when they help addicted persons develop an aversion for alcohol, drugs, or illicit sex objects. They administer repeated painful electric shock to the addict while he or she is thinking about the unwanted behavior. The effect is usually that the subject experiences an increasing desire to avoid the illicit attraction.

As we continue our discussion of a cure for anxiety, it's important to keep the role of both conditioning and misbeliefs in mind. Nevertheless, we should also remember that whether it's cognitive or conditioned, anxiety always nudges us in the direction of *avoidance.* That is, unless some overriding consideration causes us to do otherwise, we tend to avoid people, scenes, and thoughts which might invoke anxious feelings. Chauntell, for example, avoided driving until after treatment began to take effect. In the same way, we ourselves may be avoiding doing many things because we are anxious or fearful. If we are, we'll eventually find that avoidance to avoid anxiety only leads us right back to more anxiety.

How Avoidance *Causes* Anxiety

What is perhaps the most significant fact about avoidance was mentioned only briefly in chapter 2: Avoidance actually causes anxiety!

Why, psychologists used to ask themselves, don't people just get over their fear of snakes, spiders, or other people? Why do they often remain anxious and fearful for years, though they've never been hurt by a snake, bitten by a spider, or trounced by another human being? Why do animals remain fearful of a place where they've been hurt regardless of how long it's been since the harm was done? Why don't people and animals find their anxiety just fading away like grief or enthusiasm or anger or other emotional reactions?

For a long time both psychologists and victims of intractable anxiety puzzled over this question. At last, in the early 1950s, some experimenters working with dogs discovered what appeared to be the answer.[5] When an anxious person manages to avoid an encounter with an anxiety-eliciting stimulus, the anxious feelings diminish. This reduction in discomfort operates psychologically as a reward or reinforcer.

When any response is followed by a reward, it becomes more likely to occur again. It acquires a stronger hold on one's habits. So avoidance actually works to strengthen and perpetuate anxiety and to prevent a person's getting over it.

All those operations we read about in chapter 2—the activities we engage in to keep ourselves non-anxious and as comfortable as possible when we're threatened by anxiety—reduce the intensity of our anxiety *for the moment*. But in doing so, they actually make our anxiety last longer. So the very measures we usually take for relief have the longer-term effect of increasing and maintaining the anxiety!

Faith Saves Us From Anxiety

The anxiety/avoidance/more anxiety cycle can be broken. The way out is faith! If we invoke that "living, busy, active" faith Martin

Luther discovered, we can take effective measures to cure our fear on two levels.

First, we can invoke our faith by telling ourselves truths instead of the lies we've been telling ourselves. Misbelief tells us: "If you don't manage to avoid that awful thing, it's bound to happen (overestimating the probability of a bad outcome); and if the awful thing does happen, it will be so appalling you won't be able to handle it and it will devastate you (overestimating the harmfulness of the outcome)." On the other hand, faith, correct belief, says: "The awful thing probably won't happen; and even if it does, you will, because of God's promise, get through it and come out on top."

Faith is able to say these things because they're absolutely true, and they're true because they rest on the Word of God, who does not lie. God has said that, unless for some reason He can use the awful thing to do you good, He will prevent it, even though a thousand others around you encounter it (see Psalm 91:1-10). Furthermore, even if He permits the awful thing to occur, He absolutely guarantees that it cannot destroy you but that, on the contrary, He will use it to accomplish good for you (see Romans 8:28). "So," says faith, "you don't have to avoid the situation or the person or the thought you now fear."

On the first level, then, faith counters misbeliefs and provides true self-talk, which will change our feelings, lessen our fear, and galvanize us into new action. Meanwhile, on the second level we find faith operating in its "living, busy, active" manner. Faith doesn't stay in our head and in our self-talk, but it issues in actions, "good works," as Luther calls them.

Faith will always prompt and urge us to go ahead and do our duty in spite of our fears. So by actually facing our fear, and doing our duty regardless of our impulse to avoid doing what we ought to, we find that faith causes us to do what will, in the long run, cure our fears—though in the short run it may create some discomfort.

A word about this discomfort. Most of the time, the discomfort caused by anxiety isn't terribly great. Most people feel some low level anxiety about many of the things they do, especially if they lead lives that are interesting and challenging. Occasionally, however, a person of faith has to face down enormous fear, even fear in a situation where the danger is not overestimated.

The Bible tells us that some believers, prompted by their living, busy, active faith, have been tortured, suffered mockery and scourging, served prison terms, gone into lions' dens and white-hot incinerators, fought in dangerous battles or allowed themselves to be stoned, killed with the sword, and sawn in two (see Hebrews 11:18–38). Even when the danger is real and the fear proportionate to the hazards of the situation, there are times when the action prompted by faith will be to march right on into the face of the threat! Those are times when marching forward into danger is our duty.

At those times, truthful self-talk will say, "I know there's real danger here, and I may be harmed or even killed. But my God is able to prevent anything from harming me, and if He so chooses, not a hair of my head will be injured. If He doesn't so choose, I can be positive that He knows exactly how He will turn it all into the greatest good! So I'm going to do my duty anyway, even if I'm afraid!"

The Bible tells us, for example, that Shadrach, Meshach, and Abednego repeated their own faith-filled self-talk to an amazed King Nebuchadnezzar in a situation like this. When the king ordered them to commit idolatry on pain of death by incineration, they refused to obey him. They knew their duty to God and resolved to do it, though they were well aware that no oriental monarch worth his crown would shrink from carrying out the death penalty, and that it was within the realm of possibility that God would allow them to burn to death. What they had said to themselves they said publicly: "If we are thrown into the blazing furnace, the God we serve is able to save us from it. . . . But even if he does not, we want you to know, O king, that we will not serve your gods or worship the image of gold you have set up" (Daniel 3:17–18).

Exposure to "the Bogeyman"

Experiments with anxiety have shown that the one ingredient that cannot be omitted from any treatment for anxiety is *exposure to the thing feared.* One way or another, all effective contemporary treatments (except medication) involve exposing the anxious person to the thing he or she would much rather avoid, whatever it is. In the case of Chauntell, for example, I used a treatment which involved exposure through imagination. She practiced imagining herself driving in snowy conditions until she stopped feeling uncomfortable. Then she actually did the activity—driving—that she had been avoiding.

If we've been avoiding some duty because of anxiety, we need to let our faith tell us the truth. We must not continue to entertain catastrophizing and threatening misbeliefs we've been stuffing into our thoughts. In addition, we need to let our "living, busy, active" faith loose by exposing ourselves to the very thing we fear—until we can finally go and do it.

Next we'll see how to apply these two healing thrusts of faith to anxieties of various kinds.

The "Disguises" of Anxiety

I don't think my grandmother would ever have used the word "anxiety" to describe her feelings. She probably would have just called herself a "cautious" person. But I clearly remember her anxieties about our health.

Grandmother lived with us while my sister Marian and I were growing up, and her warnings resounded daily in our ears when we went out the door: "Be careful!" "Put on a sweater so you won't catch cold!" "Come right in the house if it rains!" "You can't go swimming today; it's not warm enough. You might get sick."

To be fair, I should note that many folks in her generation who had seen epidemics ravage their communities were probably conditioned to a certain extent to fear disease. In any case, it's a miracle of grace that neither my sister nor I are perpetual nervous wrecks. Yet I doubt that my grandmother would have recognized her problem as a kind of anxiety.

Many anxious people like her aren't aware that their difficulties add up to anxiety. Sometimes the anxiety is so disguised they don't recognize it, and neither do their friends and loved ones. It's hard to pin down because it can come in many forms.

In some people, anxiety appears as worrying, obsession, or even compulsion. In others, it's sheer bodily distress, and in most people (especially those who say they have little or no problem with anxiety), it appears as various tactics enabling the person to avoid the uncomfortable feelings of anxiety without actually solving the problem.

Whatever its form, anxiety is at its core a deep sense that something is wrong. It's a conditioned way of looking at life that expects the worst to happen—and tries to avoid what it dreads.

Three Faces of Anxiety

Anxiety can wear three different faces, and every one of them attacks faith in its own way. *Mental* anxiety finds its central arena in the mind. *Somatic* anxiety is manifested in the body. And *avoidance* is revealed in our behavior as we try unsuccessfully to escape our fear.

Mental Anxiety

Mental anxiety most often takes the form of worry. Worriers make themselves miserable by endlessly telling themselves threatening thoughts. Sometimes these thoughts persist in repeating themselves in spite of all the worrier's efforts to be rid of them.

What do worriers tell themselves over and over, endlessly? Here are some samples of worrying self-talk. Pay special attention to the "can't win" quality of it, the *future-rather-than-present* orientation, and the location of the distress in thoughts rather than *pit-of-the-stomach-fear* feelings.

- "I just know someone is going to break in to our house and steal our belongings while we're on vacation. The next-door neighbors had their house trashed last summer. Their TV, computer, silverware, and other valuables were all taken. I'll never have a minute's peace all the time we're gone!"

- "What if Rob's canoe tips over in that icy water? He'll die of hypothermia. I wish he wouldn't go with those other boys! They don't look to me like they're very cautious!"

- "I'm afraid I might commit the unpardonable sin. I've had some thoughts that *could* be blaspheming the Holy Ghost. I wish I could be sure I was saved! But I can't. Sure, my pastor tells me I have no reason to worry. But what if he's wrong?"

- "What if I lose my job? I know my boss says I'm doing all right, but maybe she's only trying to keep me from knowing that she plans to let me go at the next review. What can I do?"

- "I'm afraid I won't pass my final exams. Then I'll have to take another semester in school, and if that happens, I'll run out of money and won't be able to study as much because I'll have to get another job, and . . ."

- "This pain in my side—what if it's cancer? It's got to be something critical, and I'm afraid to go to the doctor because he might tell me how grave the problem really is. But if I don't go, it might get worse. I don't know what to do!"

- "If I just go ahead and finish my doctoral thesis, I won't have anything to do, and then I'll be miserable. If I don't finish it, I'll be seen as a failure. What should I do?"

- "My girlfriend wasn't home when I called her. I'm sure she's out with another guy. What if she leaves me?"

Worriers typically hear the truth in church or read it in the Bible, but then forget it in the face of their anxieties. Instead of speaking the truth to themselves, they turn their threatening thoughts over and over in their minds. They make mental lists of things that could go wrong and rack their brains for possible provisions they might make against future calamities. They practice expecting the worst, thinking that at least they won't be shocked when the worst actually happens. Many of their thoughts begin with the words "what if . . . ?"

A second form of mental anxiety that resembles worrying—except that the thoughts seem more irrational and more persistent—is *obsessional thinking*. Discussion of obsessions and their treatment is beyond the scope of this book. If you believe your mental anxiety takes this more extreme form, you should consult with a psychologist or a physician.

Whatever its intensity, mental anxiety throws a wet blanket on happiness. The evidence shows that, contrary to most people's assumptions, it doesn't matter much whether we're rich or poor, sighted or blind, pretty or plain, clever or dull, agile or paralyzed, even brain-damaged: We're happy when we're content with our circumstances, and contentment comes from living in the present.

Worry, on the other hand, keeps our thoughts either on the past or the future. It rivets our attention on the possible disasters the future may bring. And for evidence that harm lies ahead, it refers often to the negative aspects of the past, insisting that things have usually gone bad for us or reminding us of what we did to make a mess of every situation.

For example, the person we quoted earlier who worried about his house being burglarized was unable to focus on enjoying the present: a hard-earned vacation. Instead, he focused his attention on the awful possibility of coming home to a disaster. And he drew "evidence" for the likelihood of that disaster by dwelling on his neighbors' experience in the past.

A Childhood Pattern?

Though scientists don't know all the causes of worrying, they believe some people may be worriers because they grew up with unpredictable parents who were sometimes sick, or sometimes explosive, or just violently angry. Occasionally one or the other parent might withdraw into a headache or a bout of drinking. As children, this group of budding worriers told themselves they'd best not make waves. Instead, they concluded that if they could only think ahead to anticipate what might set off the problematic authority figure, they could forestall the sick headache or the drinking bout or the awful explosions. Thus they developed the habit of expecting the worst before it happens.

Whatever the source of the worrying pattern, it's clearly counterproductive. Surprising though it may seem, people often worry about things they could fix if they weren't so given to avoiding the objects of their anxiety. I mentioned earlier a woman who worried about being unable to have a baby. But she wouldn't take fertility medications because she believed that if they failed, she wouldn't be able to tolerate the apparent hopelessness of her situation. She could have set her worrisome heart to rest if she had tried the medicine with good results.

Many people like her, when they face a possible problem, take an avoidance tactic that prevents the problem from ever being solved: "I don't want to know what my teenager does when he stays out so late. I might discover something dreadful." "I'd like to go to college, but I'm afraid I couldn't pass the entrance examinations, and I couldn't stand failing!" "I'm afraid to go to the doctor because he might confirm my worst fears, and that would destroy me!" In each case, avoidance assures that the problem worried about will continue or grow worse.

Somatic Anxiety

Some people are more scurriers than worriers. They might think they have a problem with their "nerves," or they may think of themselves as "jumpy" and tense, suffering more from fear generated by their own state of arousal than from worries about life situations. They may wonder if they have heart disease because their heart pounds when they're upset; they become terrified with physical symptoms like shortness of breath, lightheadedness or dizziness, trembling, or weakness.

Occasionally, the anxiety feelings escalate because of the alarmist self-talk that often accompanies this kind of anxiety. No doubt when we're anxious, we're often so taken up with the unpleasant feelings in our body that we don't even notice our self-talk. But if we try, we can tune in on it and recognize the role it's playing.

Unlike that of the worrier, the self-talk of the somatically anxious person focuses on fears about what's happening to him or her right now. It might sound like this:

"What could be happening to me? I wonder if I'm dying. My heart's racing and I have these funny feelings in my head. I must be having an attack of some kind. Something terrible is about to happen to me. I need to get help right now!"

Or it might sound like this:

"I must be going crazy. If this keeps up, I'll be locked up in a mental hospital. And then what will people think? I can't let anybody know about this, but I need help. What can I do? What if I'm losing my mind?"

Another kind of somatic anxiety occurs in people who transform anxiety into physiological illnesses of one kind or another. Many tension headaches, backaches, muscle pains, chest pains, stomach and intestinal maladies, even elevated blood cholesterol and high blood pressure are sometimes simply somatic expressions of anxiety. An extremely important step in determining whether this is the case is a thorough examination by a competent physician. Only by ruling out physiological causes can we determine whether medical symptoms might result from tension.

People who suffer from somatic anxiety illnesses can be helped by becoming aware that their symptoms, though in themselves medical, are in reality, signs of anxiety. So they too can benefit by carefully and systematically replacing their threat-loaded, untruthful self-talk with the truth. They can also profit greatly from systematic training and practice in relaxation.

Avoidance

The anxiety we're most likely to overlook is the anxiety we're handling by avoidance. Both worriers and the victims of somatic anxiety can and probably do develop avoidance maneuvers as well to try to help themselves escape the unpleasantness. So our categories in this chapter are not mutually exclusive.

What we see on the surface of many anxious people's lives is *avoidance*, their tactic for eluding anxious distress. So it's often necessary to take common avoidance behaviors as a sign of anxiety, and then delve beneath them to their source. One starting point for getting well is learning to recognize anxiety disguised as avoidance.

"I never entertain!" Lindsey said matter-of-factly, through lips pinched together to warn me against inquiring further. But it wasn't a social encounter, and Lindsey was my client, so I chose to ignore the warning. Despite the fact that her pinched lips said, "Back off!" I asked her why.

"Number one, I'm too busy. And besides, I think it's nothing but sexism for men to expect their wives to entertain like servants while they sit around and visit with the guests. I say, 'Take 'em out for dinner!' and that's what we do when we have to return an invitation. I think that's how modern couples ought to entertain!"

Perceptive readers may have already guessed that this defense was mere window dressing for Lindsey's anxiety about entertaining. The very idea of serving dinner to guests brought uneasy feelings that led her to dismiss the notion immediately. And if she had asked herself the reasons for the discomfort in the pit of her stomach, she might have put her finger on the threatening thoughts that played around the fringes of her consciousness.

What were these thoughts? Whenever Lindsey seriously considered entertaining, she told herself she might burn the vegetables, or her veal scallopini might not taste quite as good as Kendra's, or her table might not be perfectly set. And if she stumbled into any one of these or a hundred other pitfalls, she'd be criticized, a failure in the eyes of her friends.

In short, Lindsey had a fear of being exposed as incompetent. Of course, she was overestimating the likelihood of a major goof and the "awfulness" of it, but she'd really never let herself see that. Instead, she took the route of avoidance and covered it up even for herself with her seemingly justified "reasons."

From this example we can see that when the surface symptom is avoidance, determining that the problem is anxiety isn't always simple.

Consider some other complaints under which some people I've known hid their anxiety:

Thomas complained that he had no friends. His real problem was avoiding interpersonal situations because they made him uncomfortably anxious.

Patrice suffered from nagging guilt over a lie she had told her husband. She couldn't bring herself to own up to the truth because she feared he would leave her.

Richard considered himself a writer. He had plans for a great novel, but couldn't get started. "Just a procrastinator," he said of himself. Maybe, but he was also covering his anxiety. The possibility of failure made Richard so anxious, he used a sure-fire method of protecting himself from a flop: He never even tried.

Catherine let her hair go because she hated the feeling of confinement she always had in beauty shops.

Al wouldn't ride the bus or go anyplace where others might stare at him.

The revulsion Pam felt about making love with her husband caused her to have a "headache" whenever he felt romantic.

Pete turned down the nominating committee's request that he run for office because he didn't like speaking to crowds.

Carly wouldn't tell her mother she didn't want to come home for Christmas.

Josh was impotent, and blamed it on his diabetes.

Luanne made every excuse she could think of to get out of traveling with her husband, Mark, because somehow being away from home had always upset her.

Matthew seldom made a telephone call, especially if he could get someone else to do it for him. He felt uneasy talking on the phone.

Claire wouldn't visit friends who had pet dogs.

And the list could go on. Some of these people were probably unaware of the configuration of factors underlying their surface habits of avoidance. More often, though, we *are* aware, more or less dimly, of the anxiety we're trying to evade by avoidance maneuvers, though we probably don't let ourselves dwell on it.

Practically any of these behaviors or any other complaint presented to a psychologist could conceivably be a mask or disguise for anxiety—an instance of avoidance behavior by a person who hopes to minimize discomfort by avoiding anxiety. Yet the truth is that in the long run, avoidance multiplies distress.

Physical vs. Mental Avoidance

We can avoid our anxieties through two types of maneuver: physical or mental. People with phobias, for example, can usually practice physical avoidance because they can simply stay away from the objects they fear. It isn't too hard to go through life steering clear of snakes, and it's possible though not as easy for most people to abstain from riding in airplanes.

Situations as well as objects can be physically avoided. Many socially anxious people physically avoid groups, parties, and gatherings where they might be expected to chat informally with near strangers. Some who fear that they can't perform adequately in making love to their spouses try every way possible to avoid sex. When being evaluated is a great source of anxiety, some people find ways to stay away from sports, tests, performances, and other situations where they may be judged by others. Those who fear bodily harm, disease, or death do all they can not to get into situations where risk may seem extraordinary.

On the other hand, our avoidance can take a mental rather than a physical route. In mental avoidance, we typically tell ourselves, "Try not to think about it." If we're anxious about something we could or should be doing, we may control our thoughts so they wriggle evasively around the subject or simply change the subject. We might even control others by telling them not to talk about the subject because it makes us nervous when it comes to mind.

As with physical avoidance, we can temporarily avoid feeling the unpleasantness. But the long-term effects of mental avoidance can be worse: We may warp our ability to use our mind as well as cause the anxiety to spread and intensify. Spiritual damage may result as well: To practice mental avoidance, we must turn off the urgings of our faith toward the performance of whatever duty is connected with the anxiety.

Mental avoidance can take many directions. We turn the music up louder until it dynamites our mind so we don't think about our troubles. We change the subject before the conversation we're in runs to the subject we're afraid of. We skip the obituary column when we read the newspaper to keep from facing anxiety about our own mortality.

We go to a church where the preacher condemns "negative" speech and preaches only about the positive, so we won't be reminded of realities which beget uneasiness. We put off visiting the sick because it reminds us that one day we too may have cancer, heart disease, or some other fatal illness. We ignore the poor, the homeless, the mentally ill, the dying, the divorced, the deserted—all part of the strategy of mental avoidance, of dodging the reality of their plights so we won't have to face our own fears.

Clearly, avoidance can take so many forms we may not recognize the problem immediately: some kinds of introversion, especially when the introvert dodges important contacts with others; some kinds of sexual disorders, especially when the person shrinks away from making love with a spouse because of fear of poor performance; some kinds of dislike for sports and games, especially when the person refuses to risk looking bad or losing; some refusal to engage in certain pursuits; a determination not to take certain routes; not working, not going to school, not meeting new people, not speaking up when it's our duty to do so. These may in some cases all be examples of avoidance due to anxiety. Often even friends don't discover the anxiety because we keep it so well hidden.

A Personal Anxiety Inventory

Try using the following anxiety inventory to assess your own personal anxieties. Pay particular attention to your possible avoidance behaviors. Check items in the list below that cause you to feel any amount of fear, or which you habitually avoid:

_____ heights	_____ dirt
_____ sight of blood	_____ mice
_____ dogs	_____ tests
_____ spiders	_____ meeting new people
_____ speaking in public	_____ dead bodies
_____ hospitals	_____ driving automobiles
_____ cats	_____ money
_____ disapproval of others	_____ talking on telephone
_____ failure	_____ confronting people
_____ rejection	_____ lovemaking with spouse
_____ anger of others	_____ criticism
_____ paying bills	_____ doctor visits
_____ heart skipping a beat	_____ dental visits
_____ thunderstorms	_____ injections
_____ fainting	_____ mistakes
_____ appearing nervous	_____ snakes
_____ loss of control	_____ fire
_____ closed places	_____ open spaces
_____ elevators	_____ crowds
_____ being in charge	_____ water
_____ flying	_____ sharp instruments

Did you remember to check items you *avoid* as well as those that make you feel anxious when you think about encountering them? Most people will have checked some of the items. Some will have checked them all. Perhaps you've even thought of some fears not listed in the brief inventory above. If you have, note them here:

_____

_____

_____

_____

As you work through the remainder of this book, keep turning back to this page to keep your focus on your own anxieties and their specific ways of preventing you from exercising your faith by doing what God calls you to do.

Beneath all behavior is a spiritual groundwork. In the next chapter, we'll dig down to find the spiritual basis for anxiety and for the avoidance of our duty, which impairs faith.

Chapter

5

The Spiritual Roots of Anxiety

You may have asked yourself, "Why do I have to suffer so much distress from pointless anxiety?" Maybe you've even put that question to others who ought to know something about it.

If you asked a counselor why you react to life in this way, the answer depended to a great extent on the counselor's training and theoretical orientation. As we noted before, some psychologists believe it's because you were brought up in a home laced with insecurity by parents who kept you on edge with their unpredictable and frightening behavior. Others think you probably acquired your anxiety by learning it, sometimes almost by accident. Lately, some evidence has even emerged suggesting that you inherited a tendency to be "nervous."

On the other hand many counselors—including me—would point you to the present rather than the past. We would suggest that, however you acquired your anxieties, you are *now* maintaining them through self-talk of threatening misbeliefs and tactics of avoidance.

Does Anxiety Have Spiritual Causes?

You may find all these explanations helpful and correct as far as they go. Or they may not fit your situation at all. You might say, "But I had a caring mother and a loving father. I can't think of anything about my family of origin that would make me grow up anxious! So far as I know, I never went through any more traumas than anyone else. And if I'm anxious because of *misbeliefs*, where did I get them?"

If none of the above psychological theories about the causes of anxiety seem to fit you, you may still puzzle over what's at the bottom of your troubles. As a Christian, you may even suspect that spiritual factors have something to do with your anxieties. And you may conclude that you need to understand and take into account some relevant spiritual realities.

I agree. Spiritual determinants can often be found lurking beneath puzzling enigmas in our psychological functioning. *But this doesn't mean there's no truth to psychological formulations that trace anxiety to certain learning experiences or to a person's upbringing or genetics.*

The power of learning to influence behavior has, in my view, been amply demonstrated by scientists and is well attested in Scripture.[1] Yet explanations based only on psychological formulations, useful though they *may* be occasionally, fall far short of offering an ultimate explanation for maladaptive anxiety and avoidance.

They also fail to explain why parents should behave so unjustly toward their children as to generate anxiety disorders in them. It might be urged that it's because of *their* parents, and so on back through the generations. But there are many reasons why continually blaming the previous generation is unsatisfactory. Among them is the stubborn fact that the origin of twisted behavior in the first parents is still unexplained.

If you're like most thinking people, then, you can't escape the conviction that we're dealing here with more than ordinary natural causes. There has to be a deeper reason why we go through life in untrusting fear and insecurity even when we're told over and over again that God is in charge of our lives for good. We must locate a deeper set of causes if we are ever to understand the persistence of anxiety and the perversion of avoidance.

The Difference in the Psychology of the Christian

The first step in that understanding is to grasp that the Christian psyche is different in several extremely important features from the psyche of an unregenerate person. In fact, as described in Scripture, the Christian is psychologically more *complex* than the secular person because Christians have *two* natures, not just one.

Our New Nature (Personality)

Of primary significance here is the *new* personality—fresh, alive, empowered by the Holy Spirit, in touch with God, incapable of death. This new nature is determined to walk by that faith which enjoys serving God and doing nothing but His will.

As Christians, we've already experienced the activity of this new personality in our own mind and heart. We've "heard" it urging us to tell ourselves the truths of faith instead of the lies of unbelief. This new personality knows the truth, harbors right beliefs rather than misbeliefs, and promotes the truth in our thoughts. Given a chance, it will overcome our anxiety so we stop hiding away from doing our duty. So this new personality can diminish and finally do away with those handicapping, unreasonable fears.[2]

One day, in heaven, this new personality will be all that's left of any of us. The complications due to the old personality and its misbeliefs will be gone for good.

The "Old" Nature (Personality)

But that day is in the future. At the moment, we're stuck with a remnant from the past: an old nature or personality, often called "the flesh" in Scripture. This old nature is just as dedicated to opposing God and promoting the devil's program as the new personality is to loving and trusting God.

We've also "heard" the voice of this personality, urging us to be afraid, to preserve and protect ourselves by avoidance of the duties to which our faith summons us, and to doubt seriously whether God can be trusted to do an adequate job of defending us against harm.

According to the Scriptures, we have been crucified with Christ and have died to this old personality. So we no longer have to be its slave, doing what it commands without much thought. Yet even though *we* are dead to its dominion, the flesh still makes every effort to influence our thoughts and behavior with its misbeliefs in order to persuade us to agree with it and to carry out its unhealthy program (see Romans 6:1–4).[3]

The major aim of this old personality is to push us to live in unrestricted *independence* from God. But we were created for *absolute dependence* on God. Just as every automobile is made with a tank which needs gasoline to run, every human being was made with a psyche unable to operate properly without the Holy Spirit living inside.

When God breathed the Holy Spirit into the nostrils of the first human being, he came alive spiritually. That first man was simple, not complex. He had only one nature, a living spirit, able to live, think, walk, talk, and breathe freely under the sweet prompting and guidance of God's own Spirit resident within.

Human beings were thus designed and built to do *nothing* without God himself. That way of living with God is the only true freedom in the universe. It's also the only security available to any of us, the only total safety.

"All You Need Is Yourself"

The philosophy our flesh preaches to us says otherwise: "You don't need roots. All you need is yourself! Cut the roots off. You'll be able to provide for yourself. God just wants to tie you down, clip your wings, and steal your liberty, and that's intolerable. Be independent instead!"

If we choose to do so, we can tune in on our own flesh-generated, misbelief-ridden self-talk. It may not sound exactly like the stuff in the preceding paragraph, but it will push the same message: independence from God.

But how do anxiety and worries come from self-talk about cutting ourselves loose from God? Let's say we're a worrier who stews about financial security with self-talk like this: "How will I ever pay the bills? They just keep piling up! And what if I should lose my job? I'll probably have to file bankruptcy and then nobody will give me any credit. Even worse, how will I face my neighbors? It will be terrible and there's no help for it, now, is there, as long as the people in this family keep spending my money?"

How does that self-talk connect to independence from God? If we analyze it, we find that it adds up to the belief that God won't help us, we can't count on Him, and we're on our own to take care of our needs. Furthermore, it assumes that if we don't come up with a solution to this problem ourselves, our situation will just keep going from bad to worse until we're finally destroyed. By creating the illusion that we're in charge of our own life and must solve our own problems by ourselves, these thoughts paint a picture of total independence from God.

Let's take another example. Say we're quite sure God would want us to teach a Sunday school class, but every time we think about it, we tense up and feel butterflies in our stomach. We're nervous. The kids might misbehave. We might not be able to control them. We might say something that isn't accurate. We might fail!

If we stopped to tune in on our self-talk, we would probably hear all those suggestions and more coming, very likely, from the old personality. But because we're uncomfortable just thinking about teaching, we refuse the job and our anxiety subsides. We feel much better already.

See how the flesh has fought and won a skirmish by persuading us that we're on our own or God won't come to our aid? The assumption is clear: "I could fail, and of course God won't do a thing about it when I'm disgraced and embarrassed by failure." Then the flesh wins another skirmish when we decide on an avoidance maneuver in which we shirk our responsibility by refusing the invitation to teach. Note that we're not saying it *must* be our duty to teach if asked, but it *is* our duty not to avoid teaching on account of anxiety, if we feel God wants us to do it.

71

"The Flesh" Promotes False Beliefs

To promote independence, the flesh advances the false belief that we should be afraid and anxious, we should worry, because we're on our own. God can't or won't help us. This old personality indoctrinates us until we stop believing that God is faithful, on our side, and big enough to keep His promises to protect us. We then believe the best way to handle our anxiety and worry is to avoid the frightening person, action, or situation, to shirk our responsibility rather than carry it out in trust and obedience.

"*Avoid!*" says the flesh. The message may be spoken in many ways:

- "You don't have to face that now!"
- "Don't think about it and you'll feel better!"
- "Filing a tax return is too complicated for you and you could do it wrong and get into real trouble. Put it off until you can get some help."
- "Confronting Sam scares you to death. Maybe if you just treat him especially well, your irritation will go away and he won't ask you for money again."
- "Mention *Jesus* in your office? Just thinking about it makes you uncomfortable. How can you bring it up . . . ?"
- "Better just go where your mother suggests for your vacation or she'll be angry, and you know how hard that is for you."
- "Having to make that phone call has kept you upset all afternoon. Why don't you just admit you can't handle it and give up? You'll be a lot more comfortable."
- "You can't face them."
- "It's too hard for you. You just can't do it."
- "You can't go there. You'll have a panic attack, and one more of those things will do you in!"

Invariably, the flesh urges avoidance even if it means evading a responsibility. For example, Raymond, a forty-eight-year-old bookkeeper, told me he couldn't work. He was disabled.

What was the problem? For some reason, he said, he became so anxious when he tried to make entries in his accounts that his hand shook. Since he was unable to write, he reasoned—buying into the argument of his own flesh instead of the urgings of faith—he had to solve his own anxiety problem and was well advised to stay home until he felt better. Sadly enough, he was into his seventh year of staying home, without improvement.

Carlo kept on doing his work even though making calls on customers gave him such jitters he literally shook. So he carried a bottle of assorted pills with him—tranquilizers, barbiturates, hypnotics, and sedatives. He popped one in his mouth before making stressful calls. Convinced by the flesh that he was independent, on his own, and had to take care of himself, Carlo made pills his device for evading anxiety.

Wendy grew anxious a minute or two after she drove away from her home—every time. "Did I remember to snap the lock and close the door tightly?" she would say to herself. "What if I didn't? Someone might break in! I'd better go back and check." But once she checked and then drove away, again the doubts would loom, so she'd turn around and check her front door *again.* Wendy made so many return trips to try to assure herself the door was locked that she seldom got to work on time and occasionally didn't get there at all.

Wendy's actions were very likely efforts to avoid anxiety. Psychologists would call her "over-responsible" and would recognize the behavior as compulsive. They would also know that, apart from certain relatively new medications, the most productive recovery program would call for Wendy to refuse to go back and check no matter how uneasy she felt. By doing so, she would allow her faith to motivate her to go ahead to work, take care of her responsibilities, and put her security in the hands of God.

Depending on herself rather than on God was at the base of Wendy's "over-responsible" pattern. She was taking responsibility for what she needed to leave in the hands of God. Wendy could get well only by shifting from her unworkable mode of independence to a response of faith, with its trusting dependence on God and responsiveness to His call.

How Avoidance Squelches Faith

Once, a young "expert" on morals and ethics invited Jesus to discuss difficult questions with him in order to "test" Him. The gospel writer reveals that the man's motive from the start was not a faith-generated hunger for obedient action. Rather, he wanted to entangle Jesus into a paralyzing knot of "what ifs" and "well, buts" precisely in order to *avoid* taking any action. Here's a loose paraphrase of their conversation (based on Luke 10:25–29):

- *Lawyer*: What do I have to do to be living right?
- *Jesus*: God has already told you: Love Him and love your neighbor.
- *Lawyer*: Yes, it sounds simple, but I see some really complicated issues here. For instance, how am I to know precisely who is the person I am to love? My friends? My relatives? My enemies? God's enemies? Who is my neighbor?

Jesus knew the man's motives. The man was doing what we sometimes do with God's commandments. Rather than getting up to respond to God's call the moment we hear it, we put off obedience by raising questions and engaging in endless discussions of the "real meaning" of the command. It's just another tactic to avoid doing what would make us fearful and anxious.

Avoidance couldn't possibly make the lawyer a better person. Instead, it paralyzed him spiritually. Using avoidance to cope with anxiety usually involves: (1) A decision not to trust God, but instead to declare independence from God; (2) A determination to trust ourselves and to take things into our own hands, whatever the spiritual cost, in order to ease the distress of anxiety; and (3) A squelching of faith's summons to a living, busy, active life of loving God and our neighbor. So it can't in the long run make an anxious person better. The road to getting well must surely lie in the opposite direction, the direction mapped out by faith.

Consider the things you yourself are avoiding, and study the way you're following the pattern we saw in Wendy's "checking" attempt to avoid anxiety. Maybe you're staying away from church, the barber shop, the shopping center. At times, you're no doubt deciding to ignore the summons to action issued by your faith. If so, you probably won't get better.

Maybe your avoidance comes in the shape of a pocket or purse full of pills. Maybe you get sick as a way out, or develop a "handicap" with little or no organic basis. Maybe you never take a bath or change your clothes so *others* will avoid *you* to diminish your interpersonal anxiety. Avoidance takes many forms: carrying a rabbit's foot, seducing everybody who will let you, habitually rationalizing and overcompensating. Examine yourself carefully or you may fail to discover your own style of avoidance.

Great ballplayers often avoid anxiety over their performance at the plate by performing some ritual like wearing a green T-shirt or scuffing the plate in a particular way. Hall-of-Famer Wade Boggs, for example, ate chicken every day. How are such things avoidance? Their performance, irrational though it may be, amounts to the independent individual's personal tactic for holding anxiety at bay. All of these tactics involve self-talk that stifles faith's summons to step trustingly to the plate and leave the outcome in the hands of God—the One who loves us more than we love ourselves.

The Results of Independence

But what's wrong with independence? Don't we try to train our kids to become independent? Wasn't America born in a declaration of independence? Why isn't independence a virtue?

No doubt independence can be a virtue if it's independence from an evil, oppressive, or unwholesome bondage. But it's not a virtue if it amounts to telling God, "Get lost! I can manage without you!" That kind of independent avoidance behavior leads to a number of unhappy results.

First, it usually makes your anxiety and avoidance problems worse, even though it may temporarily lessen or even relieve uncomfortable feelings generated by anxiety. The self-talk of a woman named Margaret provides a good example. She excused herself from all her social obligations this way: "It feels so good to think about just being able to stay home, to be by myself, never again to have to face other people. It's a kind of cozy, warm feeling. And my nervousness is gone!"

But Margaret found the relief was temporary. Again and again situations arose requiring her to consider going out, facing others, and interacting with them. Whenever they arose, Margaret had to work them through, experiencing considerable anxiety—more than ever—when it appeared she would face a confrontation with someone.

Avoidance makes matters worse because what the flesh calls independence really sneaks us into worse bondage than before: Anxiety is reinforced by the comfortable feelings we experience whenever we avoid or escape from a tough situation. In addition, the sheer strength of the habit of escaping rather than facing situations is itself made greater. This fact, discovered in the laboratory by psychologists, is hardly ever recognized by anxious persons. Yet it's probably the most significant bit of knowledge about anxiety we could ever discover: *The positive feelings we experience when we escape from an anxiety-generating situation actually strengthen the grip of anxiety on our life because, over the long run, they make anxiety more pervasive and intense as they fortify the habits of escape and avoidance.*

In other words, avoidance—not responding to God, not facing the issue, not witnessing when we're called to, not speaking up for the underdog because it's dangerous, not going to the doctor for fear of the "verdict," not attending school when it's hard, not sleeping in our own bed rather than Mom and Dad's, not letting faith be living, busy, and active in serving God and our neighbor—makes us worse in the long run.

The final result of letting the flesh run the show makes for a rather bleak picture. Avoiding and escaping grow more and more habitual. Faith gets throttled. Separation from God moves us into a world where the real god we serve is anxiety, until finally we no longer struggle with our own avoidance and evasion, but just give up and give in, letting the enemy direct our life.

Where Do We Go From Here?

If you've gotten to that place already, or if you can see that you're on the way there, don't despair. There's hope for you, and it lies in the direction of taking courage from your faith in God to do what God is calling you to do, and then leaving the rest to Him. That bleak bondage to despair is precisely what Jesus came to save us from.

We don't have to cultivate the flesh's independence from God. By faith in Jesus as our Savior and Lord we can say no to it. If you don't have that faith now or have lost it, call on God, asking Him to send His Holy Spirit to renew and restore, strengthen and invigorate your faith, or to give it to you for the first time, along with a living personal relationship with Jesus Christ. You'll need a living, busy, active faith to face down the flesh, let go of your grip on temporary comfort, and live a life that pleases God and overcomes anxiety for good!

In case you think you can't do it, remember this: God can and wants to do it in you. All *you* have to do is take His grace and walk forward into the face of your anxiety.

Does it sound scary? Keep your eye on the reward. You don't have to do it all at once. But you do have to begin now to change directions.

Two Personalities

From the story I told in chapter 1, about my panic over a nosebleed, you should know that I have firsthand experience in dealing with anxiety. I must also admit that in the midst of dealing with worries and fears, I haven't always engaged in the kind of truthful self-talk that would have fed my faith. For that reason, I think it would be helpful to take a closer look at the conversation that went on in my psyche during that night of growing anxiety as my nose bled for the second time. It will illustrate the two natures we described as part of the psychological makeup of every Christian.

First, we should note how the old fleshly personality seized its opportunity: "I'm scared," it said. "I could die from this, but I'm not ready!" I felt the tension increase. Yes, I *was* anxious—things were going wrong, and I wasn't safe, I thought. God isn't helping me.

The new personality, enlightened by the Holy Spirit, responded: "God hasn't left you. He knows you're in need. He'll bring you through this as He's always brought you through every ordeal! Trust Him and be patient. You've prayed. Now relax." Then I felt calm as faith exercised its blessed ministry.

As I continued to pinch my nose, the flesh spoke again: "I'm afraid my nose won't clot. I'd like to trust God, but last time I prayed and nothing happened. People do die from nosebleeds; the doctor warned me about that. Sometimes people who trust God are killed in accidents and die of diseases, even when they pray for help. I can't really be sure God will keep me alive and well now, can I?"

My faith knew the answer to that one: "Oh, yes I can. I know, for instance, that God's Word says, 'A thousand may fall at your side, ten thousand at your right hand, but it will not come near you' (Psalm 91:7). Of course I'll die if that's what He wants, but if that happens, it will be good because it will be the right time. I know He'll be waiting to receive me.

"Meanwhile, the truth is, I may be able to stop the bleeding, and even if I can't, I can get help at the hospital. There isn't much chance that this will amount to more than a big inconvenience and maybe an even bigger expense for another trip to the emergency room. All I have to do now is relax and wait to see what develops.

"I'll take it step by step and receive whatever else God has provided for me. I'm in His hands and I don't have to do anything but relax and trust Him!" As my faith spoke the truth, peace and relaxation came with it.

The old personality didn't give up that easily. Next it mounted an argument from the past: "I bled badly the first time for ten hours, and one doctor failed completely to stop it. How do I know it'll be easy this time?"

Then the old personality reminded me that I'm no spiritual giant, only a weak, imperfect sinner who has broken God's law and is nowhere near as committed as a real saint. "So what makes me think God will care about me as much as if I were really holy?" it said. "And even if the Bible says He does, it probably has some spiritual meaning, and spiritual truths are fine, but that's real blood that I lost last time. Spiritual truth might make me feel good, but it sure isn't as real as running, red blood. I've only got so much of that!"

"This Will Kill Me"

Although my flesh didn't do it on this occasion, very often this old personality will try to sell us errors of fact. Here are just a few:

- "This elevator will get stuck between floors."
- "This anxiety will probably kill me."
- "I won't be able to make these mortgage payments and I'll lose my home and everything else."
- "I'll get sued and end up poor for life."
- "I've probably got cancer or some other terrible disease."
- "I probably left the water running in the rose bed and it will flood the yard."
- "I just know there are dangerous germs on this food."
- "I'll bet I forgot to lock the front door and somebody will break in."
- "Nobody will like me."
- "I'm never going to find anybody to marry me."

A common theme sounded by the enemy within is this: "I'm stuck forever in these rotten circumstances. I'll never have a better job than this contemptible daily grind I'm in now. I'm trapped in this marriage and it's going to go on forever, grinding me to powder! There's no way out.

"God? I don't see any evidence that He cares one bit, or at any rate that He wants to help me out of the situation. He probably wants me to suffer. Nothing ever changes!"

"It *Will* Be a Catastrophe"

Yet another strategy of the old personality is to buy into blatant overevaluation of the badness of what's happening. I experienced that with the nosebleed: "This bleeding is so awful it might mean I'm having a cerebral hemorrhage, and that would be a terrible catastrophe."

Examples of overevaluation from other people's self-talk:

- "When the elevator sticks, nobody will rescue me and I'll suffocate."
- "If I die from this, it will be dreadful because death is so terrible."
- "If I don't stop getting so anxious, I'll go crazy and they'll lock me up and throw away the key."
- "I just know some catastrophe will come of this or I wouldn't feel so positively ghastly."

"Make Yourself Comfortable"

Even the tactics of avoidance and escape result from misbeliefs in our self-talk. We say (or assume) statements like these: "Self-effort is what saves people. Nobody else will take care of me, I know, so I need to help myself. Of course, I'm small and defenseless, so I have to be very careful never to take any chances. I've got to save myself from anxiety, so I'm going to wait for a sure thing. I'm for staying away from anything that makes me the least bit nervous. It's vital to be comfortable. If I'm uncomfortable it means sure danger!"

Avoidance is a self-devised and self-executed remediation for anxiety. As such, where the danger is scarcely authentic, it only makes matters worse and worse and worse.

Sometimes, especially when anxiety becomes a major problem, or when avoidance becomes the dominant pattern used for coping with it, self-examination will reveal that faith has become rather inactive. "Where is your faith?" demanded an exasperated Jesus of His tremulous disciples when they terrified themselves in a storm (see Luke 8:22–25). Perhaps sometimes He says that to us, too.

That is, when we make only a halfhearted stab at examining our anxiety-arousing self-talk, comparing and challenging it with the truth, faith may make a response, but it's too weak, too passive, and too flabby to defeat the lies of the enemy. Or it becomes acquiescent and allows itself to be discredited, agreeing when the enemy says, "If your faith was worth anything you wouldn't have this anxiety in the first place!"

When Faith Wins Out

If faith is to prevail, it has to include the will to prevail with the truth against the insinuations, misdirections, and misbeliefs peddled by the flesh. For example, with the nosebleed, my faith didn't give up—though at other times, I have to admit, I too have let unbelief and misbelief have the last words, with painful results.

Faith nearly always argues from the Word of God because only there can you find unshakable truth and no false panaceas. In this situation, my faith contended that God had not stopped loving me or intervening actively in my life to give me the very best of all possibilities. It insisted that if He saw fit to allow this admittedly distressing and unpleasant trauma, He had every right to do so. Not only that, I could and would get the good out of it which His Word guarantees, so that when God and I were done with it, it would not have amounted to evil, but rather purest good.[1] At last, faith and its truth would prevail and I would feel deep peace, quiet, and calm.

No doubt your old fleshly personality might object to having to rely on the Word of God ("mere words") instead of something more solid. Just recently, for example, while I was teaching a group how to be whole through the truth of the Scriptures, a man objected. He was tired of having to keep going on the strength of *promises.*

"I want a demonstration of God's power and justice," he said. "I need to trust Him as never before, but I don't. For years I've believed His Word, but now I want to see action to back up what He says! What do you suggest at this point?"

I suggested that this man stick like glue to the Word and promises of God. In faith he needed to talk back to the lying intimations of his flesh that God "is all talk and no action."

Faith Argues From the Word

Faith, if it is alive, busy, and active, will hold to the truth that God *will* act, but it will never argue from hollow clichés. It may remind us that God has never let us down but has brought us through countless tight squeezes. It might even say that God may allow us to lose some skirmishes, perhaps to sustain major losses, yet He will turn the whole experience into a victory with eternal significance.

In any case, because faith is grounded on the Word of God and not on our own experiences—*even when those experiences have included magnificent triumphs*—it will argue from the Word of God. There we find the potent, effective facts about God and His stance toward us spelled out in words given by God himself. Through those words, the Holy Spirit works like electricity crackling through a high-tension line, coming to us with truth, welding that truth into us, calling the truth in us to life as He called Jesus himself from the cold grip of death to a powerful resurrection triumph. There, in the resurrection, God has backed His words and promises with action in that same resurrection of Christ. Faith assures us: A God who does that cannot lie.

Three Potent Facts of Faith

From that same Word faith will remind us of a number of mighty truths to defeat our anxiety-arousing misbeliefs. Among these truths, several are fundamental:

1. *God is powerful enough to do anything He chooses so that no evil is so big He can't stop it or even eradicate it from His universe if He wants to.*

We may have heard lately that this is not so, that God is very strong, but not strong enough to defeat Satan and every evil work decisively. Whether we read this in the books of well-intentioned authors or hear it from the lips of well-meaning preachers, it's still a lie and it can make us feel insecure.

So we must let our faith call us back to the truth. Christ has already defeated the powers of evil, and we share that victory by faith. We will squelch those powers (see Ephesians 6:16, Colossians 2:15, Matthew 28:18).

2. God loves us no matter how sinful, weak, and helpless we may feel.

His love cannot be limited or turned off. Even if He allows pain, it's His love meeting a need we didn't know we had. He will limit the pain to what is necessary to accomplish His good purpose in and for us.

We might have been given the idea that God is an impersonal force who doesn't really care about details like us, or that God may love certain people, but not us because we're too wicked or ordinary. Wherever we may have heard that God's love can't possibly include us for whatever reason, it's still a lie. Jesus came to show and tell of God's boundless love for the world, for sinners, and for ordinary people like us (see Luke 15:1–32, 1 John 4:9–10, 16).

3. Even if our circumstances don't change and there is no likelihood that they will, we must let God be God and go with Him, not against Him.

Even if the doctors say our arthritis won't get any better or our disabilities are probably permanent, even if we face what seem massive limitations and unconquerable adversities, and we want to change God into a kind of Santa Claus who brings us whatever we want, faith will respond that, hard as it is, God is God.

Amy Carmichael was a tireless missionary to India who had dedicated her life to serving God. One day she had a terrible fall and never again left her bed or wheelchair. But by faith she performed a most brilliant worldwide ministry; a bubbling fountain of strength for others unleashed through her subsequent writings as she poured out her amazing personal discoveries about the intimate, tender care of a loving God!

Circumstances don't look promising? Listen! Listen to Holy Spirit-given faith and live in its truth!

4. We'll never get better by avoidance and escape.

Sure, avoidance and escape *feel* better at first, but they only make our anxiety grow and get worse. We *can* trust in the love of God, even if we don't feel it. We *can* face this down by telling ourselves the truth and going forward.

Get aggressive. Don't let your anxiety whip you. Stoke up your faith!

Now it's time to get to work. If you choose to do something effective against anxiety, the first step might be to begin keeping a record of everything you encounter that arouses anxiety or every situation you can catch yourself avoiding *because of anxiety*. At this point, just make a beginning; you may not catch yourself every time. Some avoidance habits have been pursued for so long and have ingrained themselves so deeply you may not even know them for what they are at the outset.

Later, as we go along, you'll learn more about the various kinds of anxiety and avoidance. But for now, buy a notebook and record every episode of worry, anxiety, or avoidance you become aware of. Then tune in on your own internal speech and answer the following questions for yourself, making a note of your answers:

1. What is my old flesh saying to attack my faith? I need to notice both my misbeliefs of *fact* and misbeliefs of *overevaluation*.

2. By contrast, what is my new personality of faith saying?

3. Which is more effective in influencing my actions and feelings?

4. To what extent am I practicing avoidance of the whole subject so my old personality persuades me not to bother with keeping records and detecting its presence and its role in keeping me anxious and avoidant?

Tune in and become aware of what's going on inside your own head. If you do that, you'll be making a mighty beginning!

Chapter

7

Real Causes of Anxiety

A note in my box at the office informed me that Ron had called. I remembered that I'd seen Ron once, a couple of weeks previously. He was sure he needed psychotherapy for his anxiety and depression.

"Just wanted you to know," Ron's message said, "I had a physical exam like you suggested, and the doctor says I have a thyroid problem that is probably causing my trouble. He gave me some medicine and he thinks it'll take care of everything! Thanks for the tip!"

If you aren't sure why you're having a problem with anxiety, at some point, you'll have to examine what's causing it. Take Ron's experience seriously—and don't jump to conclusions! Just because you're suffering from anxiety that's more intense than most people's, don't assume the source must be psychological or spiritual. Because the cause has a bearing on the proper choice of treatment, it's important to determine first what it might be.

Let's take a look at some of the causes of anxiety, and by the time we've finished, we'll be in a better position to appreciate the need for a careful consideration of all of them before we decide what is the cause of our own.

Real Problems

Although most often anxiety *is* psychologically caused, it can occasionally result from a physiological problem. If our nervousness, jumpiness, fearfulness, or hyped-up autonomic nervous system keeps us in torment because of a metabolic, endocrine, or toxic disorder, it would be inappropriate to spend a year combing through our misbeliefs searching vainly for the villain.

I remember Jacob, for example, a client who ought not to have been referred to me for psychotherapy by his psychiatrist. As a medical doctor, the psychiatrist should have investigated whether his anxious fear of choking might have a physical cause. But even the best doctors, like all human beings, occasionally fail to practice what they know, and this very good physician simply overlooked what, to him, probably should have been an obvious possibility.

Instead, the doctor gave Jacob a prescription for anxiety and referred him to me for psychological treatment. After several sessions with no improvement, Jacob, disgruntled with both of us, consulted a neurologist. He did a proper workup and diagnosed *myasthenia gravis*, a muscle disease that can be life-threatening if it is left untreated. With treatment for the disease, Jacob's anxiety faded.

Colin was a rugged businessman who consulted me about his anxiety and depression. During his first interview, I discovered he had been given a diuretic for high blood pressure, and that he hadn't been taking the potassium supplement his physician had prescribed. Once he understood the importance of replacing the potassium leached out of him by his diuretic, he took it faithfully and his "nervous" symptoms disappeared very rapidly.

Georgia had been treated for agoraphobia (a fear of being away from home and cut off from sources of help) with panic attacks until her hypoglycemia was diagnosed. An appropriate diet virtually wiped out her anxiety.

Tyrell's chronic feelings of tremulous weakness were caused by low *hemoglobin* (not enough iron in his blood).

Now that we've considered some somatic causes of anxiety, I must admit some misgivings. Frankly, I'm afraid many readers will try to treat themselves for "iron-poor blood" or "hypoglycemia" or "potassium deficiency" because the preceding examples have convinced them that their anxiety too must have a medical cause and treatment. So please pay attention to these facts:

1. Most anxiety does not have a medical cause. Such cases as these are comparatively rare.

2. We haven't even begun to list every physical illness which could conceivably cause anxiety.

3. It is vital to consult a physician to rule out such things and not to make our own diagnosis or create our own treatment program. Remember, "He who treats himself has a fool for a doctor!"

Psychological and Spiritual Underpinnings

Most problems with anxiety and avoidance sprout in psychological and spiritual seedbeds. Here are some of the soil mixes out of which these disorders can germinate:

Conscious and unconscious conflict. Having strong reasons for choosing both of two incompatible objectives can make a person very uncomfortable. For example, Inga wanted to make a trip to the family homestead in Norway, but she also felt the prompting of God's Spirit to contribute her money to meet the needs of helpless, hungry homeless people. She really wanted to use her money both ways, but she hadn't enough to accomplish both objectives.

That's conflict. Just being "hung up" on the horns of such a dilemma can make a person anxious. But Inga prayed about her conflict, chatted with her pastor about it, and made a decision that resolved her difficulty. The anxious discomfort quickly passed.

What if a person's desires, unlike Inga's, included something very shameful, too disgraceful for that person to face? Mina wanted to run away, to escape from the burden of caring for her new baby. But she also wanted her family and friends to think well of her. Mina, unlike Inga, couldn't allow herself to face her conflict because deserting husband and child would be sinful and disgraceful.

One morning, Mina awoke unable to move her legs. No neurological problem could be found. Instead, she had a "solution" to her conflict that prevented anxiety. Unconsciously she was avoiding the whole problem of the baby by becoming incapable of getting out of bed!

Situations like Mina's were once common but are rare today. To be honest, I had to invent her story since I have never seen a patient in her situation. Even so, unconscious conflicts of other kinds may still underlie some instances of anxiety today. But conscious conflicts that the patient shrinks from resolving one way or the other present themselves far more often.

Conflicts like the following are common, and most of the time we resolve them without great difficulty: "Should I marry Carissa or not?" "I want to become a computer programmer, but they tell me the field is already crowded, so maybe I should get into engineering." "The company wants us to move to Tucson, but our friends and relatives all live here in Trenton. What should I do?" "Should we add to our savings account or buy new blinds, carpet, and furniture for the living room?" Conflicts can hang some people up endlessly and create enormous amounts of worrisome anxiety.

Conditioning. You might have heard the story of John B. Watson's classical 1920 experiment with a boy named Albert. By exposing Albert to a sudden loud noise while the little fellow played with a white rat, Watson and his associate, Rosalie Rayner, caused the boy to develop, first, a fear of white rats, and later, fear of other furry objects. Watson ascribed Albert's acquired anxiety in the presence of furry creatures to a process called "conditioning."[1]

Most people have read about the great Russian physiologist Pavlov and his dogs. Pavlov experimented with the salivation reflex that causes dogs to begin drooling when they see or smell food. He found that if he merely rang a bell just before he spread the feast for his animals, the bell soon acquired the power to elicit salivation even without food.

Since then, others have shown that ringing a bell before inflicting pain on an animal would cause the animal to exhibit anxiety the moment the bell was rung without waiting for the painful event.

In this way, Pavlov confirmed a law of human behavior: If something like a buzzer that, to begin with, doesn't elicit any special reaction (a "neutral stimulus") is presented repeatedly to a person along with something like a painful electric shock that does elicit a reaction (an "unconditioned stimulus"), then the person will respond to the formerly neutral stimulus in a way similar to the reaction to the unconditioned stimulus. So now the subject will become frightened at the sound of the buzzer even without receiving any shock.

Psychologists now take for granted that some cases of anxiety have come about through conditioning arranged not by an experimenter but by life circumstances occurring together. Most of us have experienced painful punishment in association with certain objects, persons, words, or thoughts. In this way, we may have become conditioned to respond with anxiety when we encounter similar objects, persons, words, or thoughts. So we can acquire anxiety by conditioning.

For example, Mike, a bus driver, was rammed as he drove through an intersection by a motorist running a red light. Anxiety made it difficult for him to force himself to drive after the accident. His anxiety was conditioned, and he responded well to treatment by conditioning methods.

Olivia, whom we met in an earlier chapter, was afraid to swim or even get into the shallow end of a swimming pool. She had acquired her anxiety at age seven, when her big brothers tormented her by holding her under water. Her avoidance was the result of conditioned anxiety.

I once intentionally conditioned avoidance in a woman by pairing alcoholic beverages with electric shock to her arm. She soon developed a strong desire to remain far away from alcoholic drinks because of conditioned avoidance. That was a good thing, too, since she had nearly ruined her life abusing alcohol, and though other treatments had been tried repeatedly, none had been successful.

Other people as models. Imitating the behavior of models is a well-established way of acquiring certain behavior, including anxiety. For example, when I was a college student, I chose a few people as models, usually professors I admired. I didn't decide consciously and deliberately to try to talk, think, and gesture exactly like my favorite homiletics professor, R. R. Caemmerer. Yet unconsciously I developed a behavioral style in such blatant imitation of his that my friends readily recognized what was going on, long before I caught on to what I was doing.

Did you have a parent, a close relative, or a favorite teacher or friend who was always tense, worried, predicting the worst, overcautious, a case of nerves? If so, then depending on circumstances, it's possible that you learned your anxiety and avoidance by unconsciously imitating that person.

What we hear. Verbal messages, given with appropriately frightened or frightening vocal and facial expressions, can teach people to be anxious and avoidant. "Don't touch that doorknob, Johnny," a parent may say. "It's covered with germs! You might get sick!" In this way some overfastidious people learned their needless fear of dirt, germs, and diseases.

Many other anxieties can be learned as well from hearing the warnings of overanxious and over-avoidant others: "Lauren, you can't go out of this house dressed like that! What will the neighbors think? What will people say about you? You don't want them to think your family is untidy, do you?" "Don't ever let people know your mother and I had an argument! We don't want them to think our family has problems, do we?" "Think carefully before you speak, Thomas, or people will think you're stupid!"

Hypothesis creation. Sometimes we invent our anxiety-arousing misbeliefs ourselves—or, to put it another way, we put our thinking and reasoning powers into conjunction with the whispering of the father of lies, and come up with scary falsehoods. We tell ourselves these inaccurate and inappropriate declarations repeatedly until we come to live according to them by regular and perhaps even unconscious avoidance.

To understand Sherri's complaint of anxiety around men, consider her early experiences in her family of origin and how she formed hypotheses:

What could she have done as a seven-year-old but stand by, a mute, terrified witness, whenever Sherri's infuriated mother administered one of her vicious tongue-lashings to the little girl's beloved father? Why didn't he do something—at least answer her back? Why did he only wilt and take whatever she dished out?

In her eyes, her mother's anger had to be very powerful if it could intimidate a big, strong man like her father. So Sherri grew to feel increasing anguish and fear of these episodes, worse for her in some ways than a physical beating, though she herself was rarely the target of her mother's outbursts.

Trying, with her seven-year-old mind, to put the pieces together, to understand, Sherri generalized from what she experienced and concluded that, like her father, other men were helpless when confronted by savage feminine wrath. She further determined that anger was an atrocious thing and always damaging to others.

So she became anxious, not only about her mother's bouts of uncontrolled shouting, but about her own angry feelings. She was female, so her anger, too, must be a horrible, brutal, damaging weapon, to be denied at all costs. She avoided her anger by repressing every hostile impulse, especially toward males.

As a result, Sherri's later relationships with men were strained by her anxiety. But it wasn't men she feared. It was her own imagined potential destructiveness.

Notice that nobody had to feed Sherri these misbeliefs. She generated them herself (with the cooperation of the evil one) in an effort to cope with a difficult situation.

Let's identify, then, how Sherri created her erroneous hypotheses to deal with the painful situation at home. She told herself:

1. Anger is destructive, particularly female anger, and it's especially destructive to males.
2. Because I'm a girl, any anger I feel is terrible and harmful. So I must never allow myself to be angry at a man.
3. If I were to feel anger at a man, I would be a dangerous person like my mother, a horrid creature. So I mustn't feel hostility around men at all, no matter what they do.

These misbeliefs and the self-talk which reflected them helped to create Sherri's anxious difficulties in relationships with men. For that reason, replacing them with the truth became a primary objective in treatment of her anxious avoidance of men.

Spiritual underpinnings. While *fear* comes naturally, as an important built-in warning system to protect God's creatures from real dangers, *anxiety*—the detrimental or maladaptive fear of things that constitute no real threat to us—emerges from Satan's twisting of God's straightforward and marvelous invention, the free human creature. The liar's twists, warping God's wonderful design, insert more lies into the mind to create or maintain detrimental anxiety and the consequent avoidance of obedience to Christ, the King. As a result we avoid doing what God has called us to do, or being what God has called us to be because we've terrified ourselves with erroneous self-talk.

Tune in to the monologue the old sinful flesh wants to control you with. Does it sound like some of the following?

- "You'll probably be killed, maimed, assaulted, crippled."
- "You'll likely get rejected again, and you can't stand that."
- "You won't be able to do it (or do it right, or do it perfectly, or do it up to par, or do it as well as someone else) and that will mean you're no good."
- "You'll lose and that will mean you haven't got what it takes."
- "It will hurt you."

- "You'll get all tense and anxious again if you do that and you can't stand those feelings."

As you listen to your own internal talk at the point where anxiety threatens, can you see that these notions are false? You probably *won't* be killed, maimed, assaulted, crippled, rejected, or hurt, but if you are, God has charge of you and nothing can take you out of the safety of His loving fatherly hand. You probably *won't* be unable to do it, you probably *won't* do it wrong, you probably *won't* do it worse than everybody else, but if you do, it *won't* mean you're worthless. You probably *won't* lose, but if you do, it *won't* mean you don't have what it takes. You might get anxious, but if you do, you *can* stand it.

Can you see through the old evil foe's purpose? He wants to get you to avoid doing what God has called you to do or being what God has called you to be, to get you to walk without faith and to keep your faith locked up in words, words, only words. Ultimately, this spiritually destructive, demonic-fleshly anxiety/avoidance pattern must end to liberate you to fulfill your faith! And that's what we're aiming for together as you continue to read.

Chapter

8

How Free Do You Want to Be?

In John Milton's great epic *Paradise Lost*, a defiant Satan adjusts his vision to the mournful gloom of hell. He and his evil cohorts have just been flung into the infernal shadows by the sovereign Lord of heaven. They're still insolent and rebellious even in damnation, still determined to hail the horrors of perdition and to make the most of their newfound freedom and coveted separation from the Almighty. Satan mutters to his demonic attaché: "The mind is its own place, and in itself can make a heaven of hell, a hell of heaven."

We don't agree with Satan that the mind can make damnation as glorious and joyous as salvation. But on this point, as he sometimes does, the devil came very close to speaking the truth: The way we think about our circumstances can make them seem very much like hell or heaven. Our thoughts can transform the conditions of our lives from miserable to salutary, from anguishing to bearable, and from barren to fruitful through spiritual discipline, refinement, and growth.

This is particularly true if the painful problem is anxiety. In fact, if we suffer from excessive rations of anxiety, we've already experienced the way the mind can change things in the other direction, making a near hell of heaven by revising a situation or circumstance that is acceptable, even pleasant, in itself until it becomes the stage for tormenting thoughts and sensations.

How Much Freedom Can You Expect?

If you've caught a glimpse of the freedom you can have through the truth, and would like to experience that truth-based freedom, then you're most likely eager to read about how you can turn your hell of anxiety into a heaven of security. Let's begin by having a sober, heart-to-heart talk about how well you can *expect* to become. Can you actually achieve such freedom that you overcome anxious distress and discomfort?

Not if you think that before you can have peace God must first remove all threats, unsettling events, and dangers from your life. Not if you demand a guarantee that if you just believe properly, you'll never encounter rejections, losses, disappointments, pain, or sickness.

At a church meeting I attended recently, the discussion included some dramatic proposals for major changes in the church's program, organization, and leadership. A woman who had grown up in that church got to her feet, tears streaming down her face. Then she spoke up angrily.

"Oh, this is all so upsetting to me!" she cried. "The things people are *saying*—why, they're just terrible! I want this discussion to stop right now!" She expected people to stop proposing ideas she found upsetting, believing such notions ought to be eliminated for her on demand.

You may cluck your tongue, considering yourself more progressive than she. But think a moment. Are you one of that great throng whose expectations resemble this woman's demands?

Do you tell yourself that God, other people, and you yourself must eliminate all threats, dangers, and even anxious feelings? Do you believe you must have insurance against every misfortune or you can't have a moment's peace? Do you tell yourself, "I have to worry as long as anything can happen to hurt me and mine?"

"I Insist—No Anxiety!"

Are you striving to exist in an inviolable womb as your precondition for being happy? That's how one of my clients viewed the situation.

"I must be so thoroughly cured of my anxiety I'll never experience it again," she said. "Then and only then will I try going to a crowded place again." She believed that as long as she hadn't yet managed to surround herself with ironclad protection from everything she wouldn't like, she had no choice but to make herself miserable with worry, anxiety, and nervousness. She believed she should take no risks, and put her faith in Christ to no tests whatever. She expected first to be utterly rid of anxiety as she dreamed she had a right to be.

"I Walk in Danger All the Way!"

But that expectation was utterly unrealistic. There is no way to live in the world without change overtaking us. And if we're dreaming of the day when we won't have to take risks, forget it!

Have you ever looked at any of the pictures of this planet sent from outer space? In some you find planet earth as a fragile, tiny, seemingly insignificant dot, a fleck of dust drifting through a vast sea of space.

But if earth is a dot, what are you and I? In scale, we are microscopic mites, microbes surrounded by massive forces of the universe and the atmosphere, of weather, tides, wind, water, earthquakes, droughts, heat, and cold. Disease germs swirl around us, some unknown, some only now mutating into killer shapes which could wipe us out.

Even if we take every precaution, cancer, heart disease, or AIDS might kill us. Plane crashes, murders on the streets, an automobile driver high on cocaine or alcohol, the collapse of a bridge or a building could obliterate us, however cautious we might be.

Meantime, the world is full of financial collapse, nuclear weapons, famine, poverty, slavery, hostile governments, war, explosions, fires, tornados, and hurricanes. Our heart beats because a tiny electrical impulse jabs it. What if the circuit fails or shorts out?

And then there are friends and loved ones. Any of them could die at any moment. Our children could turn against us or ignore us. Our mate might have an affair. Our dearest one could deny God or commit suicide or betray us. One day we'll surely die. There is no place to hide.

If we're trying to insure ourselves against risks, change, or other discomfort, we might as well face it: It can't be done.

Can You Live Without Anxiety?

Nor is it possible for most people to live without feeling anxious. We can't expect to succeed if we're planning our life so as to avoid anxiety totally. We can and must learn to endure it because anxiety is part of life. If it's true that we live in the midst of so many and so great dangers, how could we hope never to feel anxious? Any life that is the least bit interesting must include some anxiety if only because that life will meet often with new and challenging experiences.

All this is even more true for the Christian life. Yet I'm afraid too much wishful theological thinking instills in us the idea that by becoming sincere Christians we create a warranty against failure, sickness, rejection, and death.

Jesus didn't talk that way. He didn't say the life of a Christian would be ever so much safer than that of the non-Christian, a kind of risk-free haven sheltering us from reality between the new birth and the moment we reach heaven. In fact, He said the opposite.

Jesus warned of unpleasant consequences for those following Him, like persecution, rejection, the cross. He said we must deny self with its security blankets (see Mark 8:34, 10:21, 10:29–30). "When Christ calls a man," wrote Dietrich Bonhoeffer, "he bids him come and die."[1]

The great apostle Paul didn't tell us he breezed through his upbeat ministry without a care in the world! Paul no doubt told the Philippians, "Be anxious for nothing," but he never claimed to have achieved an anxiety-free life. On the contrary, he owned up to a life full of trouble and even to anxiety (see, for example, 2 Corinthians 11:22–30).

Instead of marveling that we feel anxious when we do, it might be more reasonable to marvel at the astonishing fact that we're not wiped out with unremitting terror and anxiety! In view of the threats and hazards of life, in view of the certainty that we must die, in view of the daily self-mortification required of us by our faith, *it's astonishing that we aren't petrified every instant!* It's surely logical for us to feel at least some anxiety. Jesus certainly did (see Luke 22:44).

Aim at Reducing, Not Eliminating, Anxiety

So what's the point in working on anxiety if we can't eliminate it? We must learn to *tolerate* anxiety and *reduce* what we can't tolerate. Instead of searching the world over for a drug, a way of life, or a teaching that, once found, will make us never feel uncomfortable again, we must aim at enduring whatever comes, even if it includes some anxiety.[2]

Jim was trying to spell out what he hoped to accomplish in therapy. "I just want to get rid of this anxiety, that's all," he said. "I get so anxious whenever I'm trying to have a conversation with a person I don't know very well, I just can't stand it. I do everything I can think of to get away from social gatherings as soon as I can slip out."

But this expectation was part of Jim's problem. As we talked further, it became obvious to me that he imagined a world where there would be no anxiety. He believed that life *should* be that way, that, as a child of God, he had every right to total security with no interruptions.

We can't be unrealistic the way Jim was. We can't tell ourselves we'll rid our life of anxiety and the uncertainties and threats to our mortal existence with which life is riddled. Instead, we must tell ourselves, "I am working to become less anxious, and God is at work in me through Jesus Christ to save me from my sins. That includes freeing me from my own misbeliefs and the anxiety they generate. The Holy Spirit daily works faith in me. He helps me replace the misbeliefs that cause needless anxiety with the truth that reliably frees me from needless anxiety."

I recently received a letter from a pastor who described himself as having an anxiety problem that was wrecking his ministry. "I avoided my pastoral duties in order to remain comfortable," he confessed, "but as I did so, I was chewed up by guilt." The pastor went on to say that since then he has learned to tell himself the truth in place of long-standing misbeliefs. Now he is carrying out his responsibilities, relatively free from anxiety and, even more important, free from the avoidance habits he had formed trying to escape discomfort. Now he feels satisfaction in place of guilt, and much less anxiety.

Even so, he didn't say he *never* felt *any* anxiety. And he probably never will get to that state. So as we move along, we need to think of our aim as lowering our arousal level, raising our threshold for anxiety, and becoming free from some of our irrational anxiety.

Rollo May, the great psychologist-writer, has argued that anxiety is *normal*, that it is the occasion and wellspring of creativity, and that we need to learn to make use of anxiety when we can.[3]

Why do I make such a point of this? Because I know so many are perfectionists who make themselves anxious over anxiety. If you aim at total elimination of anxiety, you'll then get anxious about the anxiety you haven't eliminated. Thinking that it's just terrible for you to experience any discomfort at all, you'll come out worse than you went in!

You may be saying, "I'm disappointed in this chapter. I want to read something that will give me a life with *no* anxiety. These feelings are too terrible. I can't stand them." But I must be honest with you. Once I told a prospective client he would have to tolerate some anxiety and stop trying to avoid it by swallowing Valium tablets. He got up from his chair, faced me with withering scorn, and said: "I thought you were a *compassionate* psychologist. You aren't. You just don't know what charity is." He stalked out never to return.

I felt rather bad about it. But I guess my prospective client meant to say that if I were compassionate and loving, I would have assured him that I could help him have an anxiety-free life. Yet I couldn't tell him that truthfully, because I can't, and he can't, and you can't either.

So on the principle that the *truth* is better even if it at first seems less than enjoyable, I want to persuade you to stop rebelling against life because it allows you to feel anxious sometimes. See yourself as a pupil in God's school, one who is always learning, mostly advancing, and sometimes becoming able to "make a heaven of hell" with the truth, and very often able to stop making "a hell of heaven."

If you've been persuaded that it's best to take one simple step toward anxiety reduction than to refuse to move until you have eliminated anxiety entirely, then let's go on. In the next chapter, we'll look at another simple step you can take, along with some misconceptions about it.

Washing in the River

The following conversation is typical of many that occur in my consulting room:

- *Me:* "Good morning, Mr.___. Have you been practicing your relaxation exercises since I saw you last week?"
- *Client:* "Well . . . sort of. . . ."
- *Me:* "We agreed that you would work at relaxation every day. How'd you do?"
- *Client:* "I don't remember, exactly. I, uh, I think I tried doing it two or three times. I'm not sure."
- *Me:* "And did you get at your aerobic exercises every day?"
- *Client:* "It was a pretty busy week. I really didn't have a chance to get into that yet."

These two simple anxiety remedies, relaxation and exercise, may not accomplish everything we're aiming to do in therapy. But at this point, I'm trying hard to convince my client that these activities will repay the effort expended to do them because they have both demonstrated effectiveness in reducing tension and alleviating anxiety. True enough, they're not the centerpiece of faith's program for dealing with anxiety, but they are extremely simple to do. They're so easy anyone can do them, and their very simplicity may be the reason so many who could benefit from them ignore them. Let's look at them before we go on to more difficult work.

"It's Too Easy . . ."

The Bible tells us how Naaman, the Syrian officer, traveled all the way to Israel to consult the great prophet Elisha about his leprosy. Without even coming out to meet his esteemed visitor, Elisha told him through a messenger, "Wash in the Jordan seven times."

Naaman felt his anger rise. "Aren't the rivers of Damascus better than all the waters of Israel?" he fumed. "Couldn't I wash in them?" He turned and stomped off toward home.

What an insult! Elisha didn't even show his face! The Jordan, indeed! How unlike the prophetic healings he'd heard of before!

He had expected Elisha to at least come out and wave his hand over the affected skin. But this idea was far too simple, too easy. There wasn't enough mystique involved in this homely cure.

Had it not been for a servant suggesting that he couldn't really lose anything by giving the seemingly ordinary remedy a try, Naaman would have stormed off to Syria and missed his healing (see 2 Kings 5). But Naaman finally followed Elisha's instructions, and he was miraculously cleansed of leprosy.

Like bathing in a river seven times, relaxation and aerobic exercise are easy to do, requiring only a daily decision to carry out the program. But for some people, they seem too simple, too easy. There isn't enough mystique! How much more fascinating are those expensive weekly sessions with their therapist, where they can experience developing insight into their anxiety, find its causes, and trace its origin back to primary relationships!

Relaxation—Is It Non-Christian?

Some folks believe, mistakenly, that relaxation and meditation are un-Christian practices. My home telephone rings most often when someone I've never met wants to ask a question or be referred for help. Occasionally, I'm a little stunned at the remarks of perfect strangers.

"Dr. Backus?" queried a woman's high-pitched voice on one occasion.

"Yes, I'm Dr. Backus."

She continued, remaining anonymous, "Do you use relaxation training in your practice?"

"Why, yes, I do," I replied.

"Well, that is the same as meditation, and meditation is an occult practice, so we cannot support your ministry!" She didn't ask for an explanation or wait to see what I might have to say about her propositions. She hung up, having unburdened herself of her opinions.

Unfortunately, some psychologists have in fact incorporated ideas and techniques of Eastern religious practices and philosophy into their work. They make no distinction between deep-muscle relaxation and other kinds of relaxation training on the one hand, and the meditation techniques of non-Christian religious systems on the other. But such distinctions are essential to understanding.

Deep-muscle relaxation training has its origin in the laboratory of a University of Chicago physiologist, who has demonstrated the benefits of his muscle relaxation program for numerous tension-related disorders.[1] Neither in origin nor in practice has it anything to do with any kind of religious or occultic practice.

Meditation, likewise, has deeply Christian roots. In fact, even the Old Testament encourages believers to meditate on God, His attributes, His works, and His promises (see, for example, Psalms 48:9, 77:12, 119:48). Christian meditation consists of appropriate concentrated focus on a prayer or Scripture verse to the exclusion of all competing and interfering sensations and thoughts. One of its results is the deep sense of security and relaxation that can be so important for people who are harassed with anxiety.

Both relaxation and meditation have been proven beneficial for conditions involving tension in response to stress. Not only anxiety, but some kinds of high blood pressure, tension headaches, rapid heartbeat, arthritis pain, and muscle spasms have been shown responsive to conscientious and regular practice with these techniques.

Exercise for Anxiety Reduction

Aerobic exercise has also been shown effective for reduction of anxiety. Yet for many people, exercise never progresses beyond the stage of good intentions. For those who suffer from any tension disorder, however, especially those who find anxiety making them miserable, the motivation that may be lacking in others is often present in great quantities. The pangs of anxiety provide a good reason to begin an effective, regular exercise program.

Not just any exercise will do. Some kinds of exercise do little or nothing to diminish anxiety, because they have no *aerobic* effect. For example, lifting weights, though it may have other benefits, doesn't normally provide aerobic training. Many competitive sports, though they may have other values, do not provide aerobic training.

What exactly is aerobic exercise? It's exercise that conditions and improves the body's equipment for delivering oxygen in abundant quantities to all its cells, conditioning heart and blood vessels to become stronger and more efficient. To achieve that, regular workouts in which large muscles engage in sustained repetitive movement over a period of at least twenty minutes appears to be necessary.

Expensive machines are available for indoor biking, treadmill walking, stair climbing, skiing, and so forth. But they have few advantages over absolutely free and accessible activities we can engage in with no equipment whatever. Such activities as swimming, running, brisk walking, and jumping have been shown to offer aerobic benefits when they are done at least three times per week for at least twenty to thirty minutes per session.

Walking is probably the simplest of all to begin. If you choose to walk for aerobic and anxiety reduction effect, you need to walk briskly, not meandering, for at least thirty minutes a day. If bad weather threatens, move your walking to an indoor shopping mall or a health club with a track.

Running also requires no equipment. Work up to running gradually if you're out of condition, and then run for at least twenty to twenty-five minutes three times a week with no more than two days between sessions. Again, bad weather mustn't interfere. If it's at all possible, move indoors in some way.

Other kinds of exercise, such as bike riding and cross-country skiing, involve equipment and can be readily engaged in if that's available. But the important thing is to get started. If you have any physical disabilities or illnesses, or if you haven't been cleared by a physician for an exercise program, check with your doctor before beginning and follow his or her advice.

Don't try to do it all at once. It's best to start slowly and work up to training durations and speeds gradually.[2]

What you can expect as time goes on is improved moods, first of all during exercise, then immediately afterwards, and finally, extending over the day. Sleep will become more restful and refreshing. Appetite will decrease, and weight control will become more successful. Perhaps best of all, anxiety will diminish in intensity and frequency.

How to Relax

"If only somebody would tell me how to relax!" Carl replied when I asked him if he felt tense a lot of the time. Many people, including his pastor, who had observed Carl's tension in his movements and speech, had told him he needed to relax. But Carl had never realized that relaxation requires systematic effort.

Carl chose to learn deep-muscle relaxation. He would set aside twenty minutes at the same time every day. For him, the ideal time was just prior to the evening meal. He would go to the bedroom, close the door, and stretch out on the bed. If he found himself falling asleep he was to switch to a chair, but Carl managed to keep himself awake, though profoundly relaxed.

Here's the routine Carl learned to put himself through:

1. Begin by reciting Psalm 131:

   My heart is not proud, O Lord,
   my eyes are not haughty;
   I do not concern myself with great matters
   or things too wonderful for me.
   But I have stilled and quieted my soul;
   like a weaned child with its mother,
   like a weaned child is my soul within me.
   O Israel, put your hope in the Lord
   both now and forevermore.

   Now let your eyes close. Take three deep breaths, inhaling each for six seconds, holding the breath for the same period, and exhaling slowly for six seconds. As you exhale, feel your muscles relaxing and your body gradually sinking down into the bed or chair.

2. Deliberately tense up one group of muscles, such as the muscles in your hand or foot, then let those muscles *slowly* relax. Move on to another group of muscles, tense them, and slowly let them relax.

3. You can begin with your forehead and scalp muscles, and then move on down through your entire body, tensing and slowly relaxing groups of muscles in order: muscles of the forehead and scalp, muscles around the eyes, muscles around the mouth, jaw muscles, tongue, throat, neck, the back of the neck, the shoulder-shrugging muscles, the muscles of the chest, the upper back muscles, the muscles of the upper arms, the muscles of the forearms, the hands and fingers, the lower back muscles, the hips and buttocks, the thigh muscles, the calf muscles, the ankles, feet, and toes.

4. Deliberate tensing, though not the critical part of this method of

relaxation, has a purpose. It is to help you notice the difference between states of tension and of relaxation in your muscles. Take more time with the releasing and relaxing of tense muscles than with the tensing itself. When you get through all your muscle groups, go back over them again, this time *without tensing*, just letting specific muscles relax even more profoundly.

5. Fix the idea in your mind that muscle relaxation is progressive. When it seems as though you have relaxed all your muscles, you're just beginning. Think of those relaxed muscles as guitar strings that have been partially loosened. But you can turn the pegs and loosen them even more, still more and more, until they lengthen and reach deeper and deeper levels of relaxation.

6. When you have covered all your muscles mentally, remain quietly relaxed, eyes closed, just letting your mind drift and wander, until your relaxation period is over. Then gently stretch, open your eyes, and get up refreshed, tension free, and renewed physically and emotionally, thinking to yourself, "I am content and at peace. As a child lies quietly in its mother's arms, so my heart is quiet within me."[3]

An alternative relaxation technique has been described by Dr. Herbert Benson.[4] You may want to learn this method too. Choose a quiet environment where you will not be interrupted by the telephone, roommates, or family members. Rest in a chair or on a bed. Pray Psalm 131 to ask the aid of God, the Holy Spirit, as you relax. Close your eyes and breathe very deeply three times, slowly. Count to six as you inhale, hold your breath for the count of six, and exhale slowly through your nostrils to the count of six. Briefly direct your attention to your various muscle groups as you learned to do in muscle relaxation, noticing any special tension and relaxing your muscles, group by group, from head to foot. Continue to breathe in slowly and exhale slowly, paying attention to your deep breathing. Say "one" to yourself each time you exhale. Inhale, exhale, think "one." Continue repeating this for 10–20 minutes. You may open your eyes to check the time, but don't use an alarm clock.

When you finish, remain quietly relaxed with your eyes closed for a few moments, then stretch your muscles, open your eyes, and offer a prayer of thanks to God for His aid. Return, refreshed, to your activities.

Results

What results can you expect? "I've never been so relaxed in my life," said a patient of mine just two weeks ago. She had been practicing muscle relaxation and running faithfully.

"I'm delighted and I thank and praise Jesus! Now I know how I can turn off needless tension and anxious feelings instead of just making myself more tense over them!" said one man after he had developed the habit of daily relaxation practice.

"It's like getting a night's rest in twenty minutes," some people tell me. "My resting pulse has slowed down from about 85 to 68," said a nurse who had been into aerobic exercise and relaxation for about five weeks. "I've been falling asleep right away and staying asleep for the entire night," said one man whose tension on the job had been interfering with his rest.

You will experience diminished tension and relief from stress-related tension too. And if you continue your exercises and relaxation practice, you can look forward to even more pleasant feelings of decreased tension. These physiological measures don't deal with the causes of worry and anxiety, so they're not the entire program. But they'll help. Include them in your daily routine. It will be well worth your while.

While we're on the subject of physiological tension relief, a word about tranquilizing drugs and alcohol. It has become very common for people to treat their own anxiety and tension problems with alcohol or tranquilizers. I would urge, unequivocally, that you *never* use alcohol as a remedy for anxiety, since it can create many more problems than it solves when used in this way.

Similarly, you ought *never* use over-the-counter tranquilizers. As for prescription tranquilizers, they should be used only after careful consideration and consultation with your doctor, and then usually only for very short periods. Some new medications for anxiety which have no central nervous system effects and are not addictive might be tried. If you're addicted to tranquilizers, consult a physician for assistance in kicking the drug habit. *It can be dangerous to abruptly stop using some substances to which you have become physiologically addicted.*

Conclusion

As I've indicated, it's my belief that anxiety, for some, can be resolved fairly easily by learning to manage physiological stressors. The kind of management program I've suggested will be helpful, in fact, for anyone suffering from anxiety and its physical effects.

For many others, however, anxiety has become a deeper response to life itself—almost like a computer program typed right into both their physiological and emotional "circuitry." To rid themselves of anxiety requires change at the deepest levels. For this reason, we turn our attention to what is possibly the riskiest, most anxiety-ridden step of all for the worrier—that is, learning how to lay yourself open and begin to seek the roots of fear.

Chapter

10

Laying Yourself Open

Rick was a big man. Six feet four inches tall and muscular, he was the last person you'd expect to be terrified of anything. To imagine him trembling at a simple climb to the sixth floor of a building was nearly impossible. Yet Rick was absolutely terrified if he ever found himself higher than the fourth floor.

When I proposed that he and I go higher to treat his height phobia, he blanched. As I went on to describe the treatment, he felt his stomach turn. He experienced in *imagination* the dizziness and disorientation he always felt when he was actually high above the ground. As I talked, the shattering feeling that he was dying swept over him.

To get well, Rick would have to endure all this until it ceased. Rick was willing. I call that courage.

We had already tried other, less drastic, approaches, including systematic desensitization. Rick had seen other therapists, one for nearly six years of analysis, without any tapering off of his intense fear of heights. In fact, over the past ten years, Rick's anxiety had intensified to the point where he now felt almost unable to call on sales prospects, especially if their offices were on a fifth floor or higher.

He had developed the habit of dosing himself with various kinds of tranquilizers and sedatives just to get through his work day. But his good sense and fear of becoming drug dependent kept Rick dissatisfied with his increasing reliance on addictive medications. Now we had arrived at the treatment of last resort.

So I gently insisted, "You and I will ride the elevator to the top floor of this building and simply stay there together for as long as it takes."

"As long as it takes?" Rick's voice trembled at the thought.

"As long as it takes for you to calm down and feel reasonably comfortable." It had been Rick's habit not only to self-medicate prior to ascending to upper floors but also to finish his business quickly and then run down the stairs two at a time. Now he would have to turn all that around and deliberately stay where he felt like a man on the rack. Rick was not at all certain I was right when I told him the fear would lessen no matter how long we stayed. "The anxiety will leave," I promised him, very sure of myself.

When the elevator stopped on the sixth floor, Rick clung for dear life to the rail on the back wall of the car. I had to threaten to terminate treatment to get Rick to step off. Thereafter he stood by the elevator call button, pressing it rapidly and repeatedly with all his might, with his knees knocking together, his face blanching, his eyes wide with panic, and his breathing and heartbeat racing each other for first place.

This panic lasted for about fifteen minutes. Rick was sorely tempted to get back on the elevator and give up the entire project. But I told him if he left the sixth floor, even for a moment, our treatment was over. He stayed. I was his last chance.

Sure enough, after a few minutes the signs of panic diminished. We moved farther into the hall, away from the elevator. Rick, though still uncomfortable, became willing to approach a window (a very difficult feat for most height phobics).

We stayed by that window for nearly an hour. By the end of that time, Rick's breathing and heart rate had slowed down considerably, his limbs had stopped trembling, and he was able to see that the treatment was already effective. I was satisfied for that session and so was Rick.

Thereafter, at each of his treatment sessions, we drove to the tallest buildings in the city and sped to their top floors. There we would tough it out until Rick felt reasonably comfortable. He was heroically courageous, and progress was very rapid.

After five or six sessions, Rick was reporting no more pill use. And he was experiencing freedom from fear of heights in his daily activities. Now Rick was so exhilarated, he bought himself a ticket for a short airplane ride and, wonder of wonders, he enjoyed it.

Years later, when I saw him, Rick was still free from his panic and able to venture freely into high places whenever he wished.

The point is this: *When all was said and done, Rick was cured by courageously laying himself open to anxiety.* His treatment involved a deliberate refusal to follow old avoidance patterns and a courageous resolve to expose himself to what he feared.

Christians walking in faith aren't strangers to the idea of laying themselves open. Faith—living, busy, and active—is always prompting us to walk where we may have feared to walk before. It presses us to lay ourselves open to embarrassment, insult, rejection, and risks involved in loving God and our neighbor, and obeying God's call whatever happens, knowing (even if we don't feel it) that God is our shield and reward.

Christians need to know that we don't wait until nothing frightens us before we do God's will. Rather, courage consists of doing precisely what makes us anxious! *Laying ourselves open* is the essence of courage, and it's also the essence of the cure for fear.

Recently psychologists have been talking about *exposure and response prevention* in connection with the treatment of anxiety disorders.[1] These terms refer to *exposure* to the feared situation together with *prevention* of the habitual avoidance or escape *responses* the person had developed to get away from anxiety aroused by those situations. *Exposure and response prevention* in Rick's case meant *exposure* to height and *prevention* of his old customary response to heights, which was getting away as soon as possible. In clinical terms, this is what I mean when I say that people with anxiety problems must lay themselves open to be cured.

The Student Who Wouldn't Stop Showering

A student who wouldn't stop showering was treated by a very resourceful University of Minnesota psychology professor using exposure and response prevention. Here's the story:

The young man felt a compulsive need to shower for several hours at a time and take two to three such prolonged showers every day. Needless to say, this insatiable urge to super cleanliness interfered disastrously with his progress in life. There was little time for anything else.

"But," admitted the young man, "I can never be sure I've gotten completely clean. I'm always afraid there may be a drop of urine on me somewhere—or perhaps a particle of dirt. I need to be sure I'm not contaminated with anything like that."

What did the creative professor and his five graduate psychology students do to help the youth? They moved with their sleeping bags into the patient's apartment for the weekend. They then proceeded to "contaminate" the entire place by touching everything with their own unwashed hands—walls, surfaces, faucets, dishes, everything.

At noon, they brought in fried chicken and ate it with the patient, and nobody washed so much as a finger. Meanwhile, the patient was not to shower or to wash his hands for the entire weekend.

Does this seem a little nutty to you? It wasn't at all. It was one way of applying the anxiety cure: *exposure and response prevention.*

This particular patient, hopelessly exposed to all manner of "contamination," had no options but to tolerate his anxiety until it began to diminish. Since he couldn't wash or shower (his old avoidance responses), he had to face down his fear. And he did. By the end of the weekend, the young man's showering behavior had returned to normal, and the professor and his students went home tired but flushed with success, probably to take good long hot showers themselves!

Why Doesn't Anxiety Just Go Away?

In the early 1950s some laboratory psychologists puzzled over the fact that, unlike most other responses, anxiety seems never to go away, even in animals, regardless of how many times it might have been elicited. These researchers worked until they discovered this same key principle of exposure and response prevention.

Here's how they did it. They put a dog in a box, flashed a light in front of Fido, and then delivered an electric shock to his feet. What happened? Why, any self-respecting dog, given such treatment, will jump out of the box to get away from the shock!

Repeat this once or twice and you'll find Fido doesn't stay around to feel the current again. Instead he leaves the box as soon as the light flashes, maybe sooner. Furthermore (and this is the most interesting part), the dog will repeat this early escape one hundred, two hundred, three hundred, and more times. He seems never to get over his anxiety even though he doesn't experience the shock again.

Why? Why doesn't the dog gradually lose his anxiety and stay in the box when there is nothing more to fear? Because he has developed escape and avoidance to the degree that he never stays around long enough to learn that there is nothing to fear! As a result, he never stays in the fear-generating box long enough to work up a good case of anxiety. He never finds out that the shocker is turned off.

The psychologists decided to see what would happen if they used exposure and response prevention. So these scientists forced the dog to stay around. They put a lid on the box, put Fido inside, and flashed the light. But they didn't deliver a shock.

After a few repetitions of this experience, they removed the lid, and—presto!—the dog stayed in the box even after the signal light flashed. Evidently, his anxiety was a thing of the past. By exposure and response prevention, Fido learned not to be anxious.[2]

What This Means for You

The examples of Rick, the showering student, and the dog in the box all embody an identical principle: If we want to get over irrational anxiety, we must *lay ourselves open*. Exposure and response prevention meaning *laying ourselves open to what we fear*. And this takes some doing.

The Christian's living, busy, active faith urges him or her forward. For example, you may be reading this book because your faith in Christ has kindled your desire to stop avoiding things and respond to God in spite of anxiety—or to get over your anxiety. Faith also summons and empowers us to stop the independence-based evasions we've developed to save ourselves from anxious feelings, and to be willing to put up with whatever discomfort and distress we must go through to get better.

"Do the thing you fear," says faith! Go to the shopping mall, drive on the freeway, pet the kitten, endure long periods without washing, spend free time around airports and airplanes and fly for long trips, make speeches before crowds, enter the contest, ask another person to do something with you.

Initiate. Invite. Speak up. Let others know your wishes, your desires, your feelings. Instead of faking it, show who you are inside.

Stop avoiding people and things and actions when you know you ought to reach out and be there and do the hard thing. Be willing to experience nuisance levels of disquiet and tension. Be amenable to a little sweat on your palms, a blush on your cheek, a tremor in your weak knees, a dry stickiness in your mouth, a quickening of your heartbeat, lightheadedness, tension in your muscles, and apprehension in your mind! None of this will kill you, but if you really face it and endure it, it will help you overcome your anxiety.

Worriers can follow the same principle. Don't practice mental avoidance, telling yourself, "I just won't think about *that*. It's too terrible!" Instead, go ahead and face the threats you pose to yourself mentally. Open your thoughts to the worst, follow your what-ifs to the limit.

Faith prompts: "All right, if worse comes to worst, you will lose all your money. All right, if worse comes to worst, your loved one will get sick or die. All right, if worse comes to worst, you will suffer pain or die."

If it happens, it happens, and you can and will come through it victorious because Jesus Christ will be right there with you. However bad it gets, He'll be there giving you the faith to walk through it. *Through* it, because the truth is you won't simply remain *in* it, whatever it is. There will be an end point, a goal, a victory celebration.

Whatever it is, worrier, let your mind go right through it in faith with Him. Don't tell yourself to avoid thinking about it because it's too awful to imagine![3]

"I Couldn't Possibly Do That"

"Oh, I couldn't possibly do that!" Marie exclaimed when I finished telling her about Rick's treatment success and how faith urges us to go forward.

I took her at her word. "You mean such all-out, all-at-once inundating with anxiety is more than you are willing to put yourself through?"

"Yes. I want to do the things I fear, and I know my faith urges me to do some of them. But isn't there a way to start gradually?" she pleaded.

Fortunately, for some situations, there is. If we, like Marie, are so overwhelmed we would rather try anything than face our anxiety-provoking situations all at once and stay there no matter what, we can, in some situations, accomplish the goal gradually.

Let's suppose, just for the sake of illustration, we become utterly unnerved at the prospect of having to drive a car anywhere, but driving on the freeway is so frightening for us, it's out of the question. We know, in our spirit, by faith, that God has given us many life responsibilities we can only accomplish by driving. But up till now we've been excusing ourselves because of anxiety. We know the stirring of our faith is urging us to face and overcome the barriers and to fulfill God's will for us.

What can we do? Well, one way to open ourselves up all at once would be to get in a car and start driving, access the nearest freeway entrance, and keep driving until we're comfortable—even if it takes eight hours or more, stopping only for gas. We could do this every day for as long as it takes for us to become anxiety-free about driving. This would be an all-at-once cure.

But perhaps we don't want to do it that way for practical reasons. We want to use exposure and response prevention, but gradually. How could we go about doing that?

First, we would jot down a list of driving-related situations we get anxious about. We might feel a little anxious just holding the car keys in our hand, a little more anxious sitting in the passenger seat, and even more anxious sitting in the driver's seat of an automobile. So we'd write our list starting with the easiest and work up to the hardest situation, which in our case, would be having to drive somewhere on a freeway. Then, we'd make a plan for exposing ourselves to our situations, step by step, starting with the easiest.

Let's say we plan to spend an hour a day at anxiety-reduction. The first session, like the others, can begin with a prayer of faith: "Lord, I know you want me to fulfill my responsibilities, and my responsibilities involve driving. So I look confidently to you to work in me now toward that end. In Jesus' name. Amen."

Next, we'd spend ten or fifteen minutes relaxing from head to foot. Then we would take our situations one by one and, beginning with the easiest, do each until we're comfortable. If we begin to feel tense, we'd stop and relax again. We may not get through more than one or two during a session. But that's all right, as long as we keep progressing.

First, we'd just hold the car keys in our hand and continue until we felt perfectly comfortable holding the keys. Then we'd move on down our list. We'd sit in the passenger's seat with the car in the driveway, ignition turned off, until we're comfortable.

When we feel no anxiety, we'd sit in the driver's seat, start the car and sit in the car with the engine running (making sure we're in a well-ventilated automobile and not in a closed garage). The next step might be to drive the car forward and back in the driveway. Then we might drive around the block several times until we're comfortable doing that.

Again, if we become tense, we would stop for a few minutes and enter into God's rest, repeating our prayer and then relaxing our entire body again. Continuing this procedure, we would progress down our list over as many days or weeks as we need until we're able actually to drive on the freeway with a reasonable degree of calm.

This method of gradual exposure works fine for such fears as heights, driving, closed rooms, elevators, water, animals, dirt, and other situations that are easily controlled. But it does have drawbacks. Some things people fear can't be so easily experienced in controlled doses: for example, making speeches, meeting new people, talking on the telephone, conversing with someone of the opposite sex, going to church, and telling other people how you feel.

For such situations, it's possible to achieve exposure and response prevention in our imagination instead. Rather than exposing ourselves all at once to whatever doses of anxiety the environment happens to dish out to us, we visualize encounters with our fears in small, graduated doses. Generally, it's easiest to do this with the help of a therapist, since the other person can introduce the situations to be imagined to us while we are in a deeply relaxed state, with the relaxation inhibiting anxiety all the while.

Imagination Works, Too

Rebecca, a twenty-eight-year-old bus driver, became terrified of driving following a serious collision in which another driver had run a red light and crashed into her vehicle, killing himself and severely injuring his passenger. Rebecca was taught relaxation over several sessions and then asked to picture or visualize a list of "scenes" while in a relaxed state. The scenes were, of course, all related to driving and accidents, beginning with very easy and only slightly fearful situations and working up to close calls and near crashes.

All this took place over a number of sessions, each scene being repeatedly visualized by Rebecca until she was able to imagine herself in it without anxiety. Then the next scene would be attempted. In three weeks Rebecca was driving her bus on a limited schedule, and by the end of her twelve-week treatment she was able to operate her vehicle normally and without fear.

Researchers at Washington State University in Pullman wanted to know if a similar technique for imaginary "exposure and response prevention" would reduce what they called "communication apprehension" or fear of talking with other people, especially of making speeches in public. They studied 107 students in a public-speaking class, all of whom admitted that they had communication apprehension. They divided the class into four groups.

People in one of the groups were coached to visualize the entire day on which they would be giving a speech: putting on their best clothes; feeling confident and thoroughly prepared; and giving a smooth, excellent speech. The other groups were given other forms of treatment. The group that visualized the entire day made more gains against anxiety than any of the other groups.[4]

You may be able to do some of this for yourself by listing a series of situations dealing with the theme of your anxiety. Then you can progress step-by-step from the least threatening to the most threatening, visualizing yourself in the situation or doing the activities while you're deeply relaxed. You begin with the easiest and repeat it until you're comfortable with it, and then you move on up the list. If it doesn't work well for you to do this yourself, you may want to consider seeing a Christian psychologist who has been trained to use such techniques as systematic desensitization, visualization, and stress inoculation.

Laying yourself open to your anxiety this way—being willing to encounter the things you fear, all at once or gradually, in reality or in imagination—will diminish your anxiety and may even eliminate specific anxieties.

Faith and Courage

Our point here is that faith in Christ Jesus activates us to respond to God, motivates us, and summons us to go forward even into situations which seem fearful. Faith gives courage, but courage is not defined as the absence of anxiety. Courage is going forward whether we're anxious or not.

Think of David marching in faith, his only armor, onto the field against the mighty Philistine warrior Goliath. Do you imagine that David had no anxiety at all? Don't you think it more likely that he told himself the truth of faith: "God is my protection and my shield, whatever happens," and marched out there anyway, facing his fear down?

Think of Daniel, in faith defying the king's orders against praying to God, and when the time came, walking forward into the lions' den. Do you think Daniel contemplated the claws and teeth tearing his flesh without any anxiety at all? More likely, I think, he told himself the truth: that His God was in charge; that if God chose to, He could paralyze the lions; but that if God chose not to, He could and would see that Daniel was victorious even through death.

Think of Shadrach, Meshach, and Abednego choosing by faith to face the ordeal of the fiery furnace rather than sell out and worship the king's image. Do you think they had no fear in the pit of their stomachs when they looked into the white heat of the furnace, knowing for certain that they would be thrown into the midst of it?

I don't. I think they felt plenty of fear, but went ahead in faith anyway. They told King Nebuchadnezzar what they told themselves: "Our God whom we serve is able to deliver us from the burning fiery furnace, and He will deliver us from your hand, O king. But if not, let it be known to you, O king, that we do not serve your gods, nor will we worship the gold image" (Daniel 3:17–18 NKJV).

Their self-talk took into account the possibility that God might let them be burned to death. But they knew that should such be His will, it would be made into good for them.

Think of Peter stepping by faith out of that boat at night in the face of huge waves. Do you imagine that he felt totally calm? I don't. I believe he felt the anxiety tearing him apart. But because His Lord bade him walk, he walked.

Do you see how faith gives courage? *Not*, as many people imagine, *by magically dissolving feelings of anxiety and wrenching fear*, but by giving people the motivation, purpose, and power to open up to anxiety by moving ahead into it when God calls.

Telling Yourself the Truth—and Doing It

Faith can enable us to lay ourselves open. Imagine yourself acting courageously by faith. What is it you'd like to do and are afraid to do? See yourself believing so profoundly in the love, the reliability, and the power of God in Jesus Christ that you can stand in His strength *even against what you fear the most*.

You can be enabled to stand up boldly, as Jesus himself did, to people who would push you around. You can be equipped to get up and talk in front of a crowd, to make a proposal of marriage, to ask for a date, to perform in public, to take on a competitive challenge, to compete for a prize, or to ask someone for love and friendship.

"But I'm too scared," you say. Don't look at your fear, but at God's calling, and at yourself obeying, marching ahead, opening up to and embracing the thing you fear. Whether it's all at once or a little at a time, whether it's in fact or in imagination at first, do it. That's what faith urges and enables!

Faith from one perspective is telling ourselves the truth, especially the truth about God and ourselves and our situation. Here are some basic anti-anxiety truths that faith enables us to tell ourselves: God is for you, not against you. God will bless you, not curse you. God will honor your faith, not ignore it. You are safe, secure, all right, and nothing can touch you. Even death has, for you, had its teeth pulled, by the dying and rising again of God in the Man, Jesus Christ.

But as James points out, faith also includes action. So tell yourself the truth and then resolve to begin *doing* what you now avoid because of fear. The bonus: By faithfully telling yourself the truth in faith and just as faithfully doing what you fear in faith, you will conquer your anxiety.

Next, we'll take a closer look at the truth you need to be telling yourself for healing.

Breaking the Spiral

Kevin gave a perfect demonstration of how an anxious person can perpetuate his own difficulties. Listen in, and you'll see how he fed himself misbeliefs instead of nourishing truth.

"I'm anxious, tense, jumpy, and nervous most of the time!" he said one day. "The thing I need *most* is help from God. But that's the hitch. Help from God is exactly what I *can't* have, because I'm such a lousy excuse for a Christian.

"A real Christian wouldn't be anxious like me. So God isn't about to hear my prayers. My faith is so weak and ineffective, God must be fed up with me. I'm sunk."

Whenever Kevin repeated this and other statements to himself (which was very often), he felt more frightened and anxious than before. Of course this increased his anxiety—which he then took as proof that he was out of favor with God. This further confirmed his destructive beliefs about faith. In this way, Kevin fashioned an anxiety spiral for himself, telling himself misbeliefs that caused him to become more anxious, which in turn increased the strength of his misbeliefs. . . . What he needed was truth to replace the spiritual falsehoods!

The Anxiety Spiral

Many, perhaps most, people who have a painful anxiety problem also fall into the habit of telling themselves falsehoods *about their anxiety and about its meaning.*

Consider these misbeliefs about faith and anxiety that proliferate in the minds of anxious people. These all can have the effect of spiraling our anxiety upward:

- "I must be a very poor Christian to have such anxiety problems."
- "I have to keep myself from feeling very anxious ever again because I can't stand the feelings."
- "I feel like I'm dying."
- "They'll lock me up if this gets any worse."
- "My faith ought to be strong enough to keep me from being so afraid, but it isn't—so I'm in bad spiritual trouble!"
- "Nothing I try works, and I just keep on getting anxious, so my condition must be hopeless."
- "God doesn't love me much or He would take this fear away."
- "God's promises sound good, but they don't work for anxious people."
- "God has big goals that have nothing to do with me, like getting the world converted; He doesn't care what I'm feeling now."
- "The Bible says God is a God of wrath and a consuming fire, so knowing I'm such a failure makes me more anxious than ever."
- "I don't know the Bible well enough and I can't get anything out of reading it. So I can't tell myself the truth and I won't get better."
- "How do I really know what the truth is? It's all too confusing!"
- "I could never face exposing myself to my fears. They're bad enough now when I do everything I can to avoid them."
- "I'm going to get a psychosomatic illness from this anxiety, and that's awful."

Those are typical of the top layer of misbeliefs, our misbeliefs about the anxiety itself. Such misbeliefs lead to both *avoidance* and *depression*. First, the sufferer actually increases her misery by trying to avoid the anxiety she has convinced herself is so terrible, traumatic, and disastrous. Meanwhile, the person becomes discouraged and hopeless about the future, and thus she's further victimized by the misbeliefs of depression. Then depression misbeliefs may increase anxiety, leading to another spiral loop upward.

The Key to Stopping the Spiral

Kevin learned to combat his own misbeliefs by insisting on telling himself the truth. He had to develop the "truth only" habit by first writing out his misbeliefs and then, persuasively, even combatively, countering them by writing the truth for himself. When Kevin caught himself spiraling upward in his anxiety, he called a halt to whatever he was doing and sat down to write. Study this example from his journals:

Misbelief:	Truth:
Anxiety is terribly bad for me.	Not so. Anxiety is uncomfortable, even painful, but it isn't going to kill me or drive me crazy or destroy my life, and the less I spook myself over it, the better I'll feel. So I'm going to tell myself, "I don't enjoy this, but I refuse to ring all the alarm bells."
I must be a very poor Christian to have such anxiety problems.	Why do I tell myself such garbage? I know JESUS HIMSELF felt worse anxiety by far! His sweat was full of blood! God loves me and forgives me for these misbeliefs and He is helping me right now to overcome them. That's what a Christian is—a forgiven sinner being healed by God's mercy! And I sure do qualify!

Misbelief:	Truth:
I have to keep myself from feeling very anxious ever again because I can't stand it.	Forget that trash! Of course I don't have to force myself to feel or not feel anything. I know I'll feel anxious as long as I'm here on earth. Every person who's really alive and leading an interesting life experiences some anxiety.
Nothing I try works, and I just keep on getting anxious, so my condition must be hopeless.	No condition is hopeless. I can evaluate why things I've tried haven't helped and keep working on a solution. Eventually, I'll find one because I know God isn't going to leave me in difficulties. His salvation and helping will finally be 100 percent!
God doesn't love me much or He would take this fear away. God's promises sound good, but they don't work for anxious people. God's goals aren't my goals, so He doesn't care what I want. God is a God of wrath and is a consuming fire, so when I think about Him I just get more anxious than ever.	The Word of the living God says that He loves every one of His children, that He loves the whole world, that He does not lie, and that He *always* keeps His promises. The Word also says He cares for me so I can cast my cares upon Him—even if my goals don't all match His yet. God's wrath touched Jesus on the cross and He is my substitute. I don't have to face wrath because He died for me.
How do I know what the truth is really? It's all too confusing!	God's truth is in His Word, in His world, and in the rationality He created in me. I can know it and tell it to myself if I work at it. Right now, the truth is I already know that He is on my side.
I could never face exposing myself to my fears; they're bad enough now when I do everything I can to avoid them.	The truth is I could face even more anxiety than I feel now *if I had to,* but I can expose myself step by step to the things I fear. What's important is for me to realize I need to stop avoiding my fears and instead be ready to face them and walk straight into them, trusting God to keep me.

In addition, and perhaps most importantly, Kevin learned to tell himself firmly and repeatedly that avoidance, though it might purchase some short-term relief, would in the long run only make things worse. He didn't *have* to avoid things that weren't dangerous just because they made him anxious. He repeatedly reminded himself there was no way to avoid all distress and pain, that human life can *never* be hassle-free, and that he wanted to do what God required of him, even when it elicited anxious feelings.

By insisting on these truths, Kevin was increasingly able to tolerate the idea of exposing himself to the fear-filled situations he'd always tried to avoid. He was also able to experience a welcome diminishing of his spiraling anxiety—his fear of fear.

Faith, Fed With Truth

The power to move forward in responding to God was furnished for Kevin by his Christian faith as he kept on feeding it with truth. According to Scripture, faith grows strong when you feed it with nourishing truths about God's saving love in action through Christ Jesus: "Faith comes from hearing the message, and the message is heard through the word of Christ" (Romans 10:17).

Like Kevin, we must not feed on the junk food that bloats anxiety, like "God doesn't love me much." Instead we must feed our faith with genuinely nutritious truth like this: "God loves me with an everlasting love that is unconditional, unending, undefeatable! He has acted on that love by sending Jesus to suffer death in my place. How shall He not with Him also freely give me all things?"

We must not keep stuffing ourselves with "stale bread" like this: "God's promises sound good, but they don't work for me. He never hears my prayers—never!" Instead, we need to feast on the truth that puts real muscle to our faith: "God can't lie. His promises are guaranteed by the life, death, and resurrection of Jesus, and by the powerful presence of the Holy Spirit—the down payment God has made to guarantee the final, complete fulfillment of all His words."

The truth is *not:* "If I don't protect myself, God might let me get hurt more than I can stand. After all, He can't really empathize with me, because He isn't a human being. Nothing can hurt Him. But I'm vulnerable." The real truth is: "God knows how human pain feels because He became a Man and went through it all, facing what made Him anxious and coming through victorious, all along vowing that He is my own tender Shepherd, who will hold me safe from real harm even if He allows me some uncomfortable feelings! Eventually, He will remove even those."

Can you see from these samples how faith feeds on truth? And can you catch a glimpse of the way such truth-digesting faith can motivate us to forsake avoidance, and encourage us to do God's will? Perhaps you can even glimpse the new life of freedom from excess anxiety that lies ahead through exposure to the things you've feared and avoided.

Recognizing, or Believing?

Faith, Christian faith, means in part believing or telling ourselves the truth in place of the lies and misinterpretations of reality fostered by our old nature, our sinful flesh. But one aberration we may stumble over in our healing process is the habit of confusing *recognition* with *believing.*

Two of our grandchildren, Jenny and Jacob Templeton, have lately started saying, "I know that!" whenever they're told something they think they've heard before.

"Jenny, Christmas is coming very soon," Candy, my wife, said the other day.

"I know that!" replied Jenny.

"Jacob, you've been an especially good boy today," said Candy.

"I know that!" responded Jake. As I chuckled, listening to them, I was reminded of those Christians I've seen who, instead of listening to the truth and incorporating it into their self-talk, only hear the Word preached and register *recognition* to themselves rather than belief.

The inner dialogue goes something like this:

"God loves you." ("I know that.")

"He keeps His promises." ("Yes, I've heard that many times.")

"God protects His own children." ("I know that, too.")

Instead of *actively believing* the Word—taking it in like a baby gulping mother's milk, eagerly telling it to themselves in connection with real, tough life situations—some people just give the truth a nod of recognition as it flies by their ears.

Wouldn't it be ridiculous if we did that with physical food? Imagine! You're at the table, someone passes you the bread, and instead of taking it and eating it, you say, "Yes, that's bread. It surely is. I know that." Then you pass it on.

Yet that's exactly what some of our clinical clients do with the truths that could set them free if they would take them in and start actively advertising them to themselves. Instead, when we try to show them that God values them as priceless treasures, or that He insists over and over that He *will* answer their prayers, or that what others think of them isn't the criterion on which everything stands or falls—or any other solid truth—they tell us, "Well, I already know that. But it doesn't seem to help!" They pass the bread on without eating any!

What we're talking about is not merely knowing truth, but *internalizing* it. Mere recognition sounds like this: "Oh my goodness, I've been told I have to take a plane trip. How can I get out of it? It traumatizes me to have to get on a plane.

"Yes, I know God promises to see me safely through frightening experiences, but you don't realize how terrible I feel when that crate gets up in the air. By then, I'm tied up in knots. I can't think, I can't breathe, I feel like I'm going to suffocate. It's terrible. I'd better tell the boss I have other plans and can't go to the convention."

On the other hand, *belief* would have these sufferers tell themselves, as they feed on the truth, "A plane trip? Well, might as well face up to it. If it's part of my job I'll have to do it.

"Maybe I could start by reminding myself of what God says about His care and protection. Yes, that's what I'll do. Then I might get the courage to spend a few hours at the airport, just hanging around airplanes, exposing myself in advance to the situation.

"I'm going to go right ahead and face doing what I ought to, leaning on God's Word and promises. I'm going to fly on that plane because God doesn't lie, and He loves me."

Faith Acts

Remember, faith *includes action*; according to James, it's dead if it doesn't. Especially where anxiety furnishes us with a reason for avoiding responsibility, faith prompts us to act. For that reason, we'll be aware of conflict, painful conflict.

That pain comes because our faith won't quit—it won't stop urging us, for instance, to try going farther from home even if we've spent the last three years at home because of irrational fear. That "living, busy, active faith" of ours wants to be nourished by the truth so that it may gently but firmly urge us on even when our old flesh doesn't feel like doing something because of anxiety.

I see in my mind images of real people urged on by their faith to lay themselves open to what was making them anxious by responding to God. I see Rebecca driving again and again past the scene of her traumatic accident. I see Rick making himself ride elevators for hours on end. I see Terrence forcing himself to sit in the front row at the church service. I see Jane compelling herself to imagine scenes relating to illness and death in spite of her unreasoning terror. I see Dave, having to hold his trembling right hand still with his left as he sat for examinations in graduate school. I see Lindsey resolving to invite people to her apartment, willing herself to engage in conversation with them and determinedly serving refreshments to them.

Some people may criticize them because they weren't *enjoying* all these things. But they were all profiles in courage because, even in the face of terror, they allowed their faith to motivate them toward what they believed God willed for them to do.

Stop Avoiding—You Aren't on Your Own

If we continue telling ourselves it's up to us to protect ourselves against fearsome feelings, avoidance habits may increase until they nearly ruin our life. I've known people who, by avoidance, eliminated friends, mate, job, and every conceivable success from their lives. Moreover, they perpetually felt guilty because they wouldn't stop avoiding whatever made them uncomfortable.

Occasionally, being known as a Christian psychologist gets me invited into some strange and difficult situations. Some people find it hard to understand how anyone could be a believer in the Bible and at the same time a respectable psychologist.

I once found myself, for example, on a platform at one of our state universities, preparing to speak to a manifestly hostile audience of students, professors, and psychologists. The talk had to do with Christianity and psychology. As I sat in the auditorium waiting to be introduced, I began to think about the audience and the strident secularism permeating the university campus, the closed minds, the acerbic sarcasm with which many would phrase their comments later.

The low-level anxiety I'd brought with me spiraled! Panic struck, my heart pounded, my breathing felt shallow and insufficient, and my knees were weak. *What am I doing here?* I wondered. *Why on earth did I accept this invitation? I can't handle this. How do I get out of here?*

But there was no way out. . . . I told myself God wanted me there doing this or He wouldn't have had me there, and that He was there with me. I told myself that if I fell flat on my face or collapsed from anxiety, I'd just have to go through it, but I wouldn't have to face it alone.

I heard myself being introduced, got to my feet, walked to the microphone, and barely thinking about what I was saying, began my talk. But now I forced myself to focus not on the anxiety but on what I was saying. I concentrated on the important facts I was bringing these people, that God worked in and through the psychological laws they were investigating every day, and that God had something to say about human behavior beyond those psychological laws—something called "the law of the Spirit of life in Christ Jesus."

The more I concentrated on doing what I was there to do, the less nervous I became. Soon I was relaxed, comfortable, and thinking clearly. Even when I had to field some rude interruptions, severely critical comments, and rather hostile questions, I was able to keep cool and to respond amiably and truthfully.

Why? What happened?

Several elements were involved that merit noting here:

- *Exposure.* I made myself walk straight into the anxiety! I was exposed for an hour to the feared situation and nothing dreadful happened. So it began to be obvious that for me, as for Solomon and Wynne's dog in the box, nothing was actually going to hurt me after all.

- *Truth.* I told myself the truth about God's promises and about the negligible likelihood that even if worse came to worst I would suffer disaster. "You are not on your own," I told myself, "no matter *how* it feels. Jesus Christ said He would be with you always, and He doesn't lie."

- *Focus.* Instead of concentrating on my anxiety and panic with all the threatening thoughts that could have run through my mind, I focused with all my might on my speech material, on presenting it, and on my effort to persuade. After all, what I had gone there to do was, both to me and Jesus, important—more important than my anxious feelings.

Sometimes it helps to sift the nonessentials out of our self-talk.

When we do that in a fearsome situation, we must come right down to the major question: *Are we on our own?*

If we are, then it's vitally important for us to be charming and clever in every social setting. It's critical for us to learn skills of self-protection, manipulation of others, even deception where that's necessary. We must also deceive ourselves at times. If we're on our own and we don't have these and other significant attributes; if someone else has us beat; if we can't be sure we'll perform stunningly, win everybody's approval, and appear calm and unruffled while doing it; then we lose. We can't win. So we'll conclude that we have to preserve ourselves by avoidance of anything we can't be sure of doing safely without anxiety.

But on the other hand, if we're not on our own, we're living by faith. Never being on our own, never independent, but always dependent on God, we can walk straight into the midst of what frightens and challenges us. We can take a chance on finding out how really terrible it would be if our worst fears came true, because even if they did, we wouldn't have to go through them alone. God would be with us. For that reason, we can pay attention to doing whatever it is we're doing— and to doing it as well as we can because we're doing it for the God who has called us and fills us with the faith to obey Him.

"Even If . . ."

Try playing "even if" with yourself. Tell yourself truths like these:

- "Even if I found someone disliked me, I would still have my Lord's favor by faith!"
- "Even if I discovered that somebody criticized me, or got angry at me, or gossiped about me, I would be in good company, because Jesus experienced those same events and came through with flying colors. So maybe I could too!"
- "Even if I were to get lost en route to somewhere, I would survive

because I wouldn't be alone. My Lord has promised to be present with me always."

- "Even if my car broke down on the freeway or the elevator got
stuck or I panicked in the middle of the shopping mall—even if
all those things happened—I would be supported through it and
enabled to deal with it by my Lord!"

When we take the "badness" with which we've always threatened
ourselves and hold it up to the light of the truth as it is in Jesus, then
we find that God's love, promises, and caring can reveal the worst to
be endurable and conquerable through Him. Even death has no sting
when seen with the eyes of faith.

Like Kevin, then, you may begin your faith attack on anxiety by
keeping a notebook. Start noticing your avoidance behaviors. Then note
what you could do by faith and what you would need to tell yourself
in order to do it.

Finally—plunge ahead! Expose yourself to the thing that scares you.
Focus on what you're there to do and on doing it well. And feed yourself
on the truth about God's promises. They will never fail.

Chapter

12

Exploding Your "Myth Beliefs"

Let's say we've thrown out the misbeliefs that buttress avoidance behavior, including the misbeliefs about anxiety itself and how awful it is to feel anxious. Let's say we've peeled away the avoidance layer, and made a bold advance into new territory. We've begun to trek across a new landscape.

At this point, then, that top layer of misbeliefs no longer works against us, because we've replaced falsehoods with truth. But a second layer is usually still in place. Even so, we're determined to press on because that living, busy, active faith of ours has gently but firmly urged us to respond to God in the situations we previously avoided. So we must now explore the level of what I call "myth beliefs."

"Myth Beliefs"

This part of the project involves getting in touch with the *underlying* layer of beliefs and self-talk by which we make ourselves so keyed up. These are the misbeliefs that *cause* anxiety, but they aren't *about* anxiety. They are usually about events that never happen.

Once we've uncovered these myth beliefs, these erroneous notions undergirding our fear, we'll need to become convinced that they're false and tell ourselves the truth in place of them. Here we come to the heart of what faith is: not a static subscription to doctrines (although doctrines are important), but believing in an active, involved, participatory manner, and *actively, aggressively approaching everything in life on the basis of truth.*

When faith is living, busy, and actively promoting the truth, it will give us victory over the anxiety pushed on us by the world, for "this is the victory that has overcome the world [with all its anxiety], even our faith."[1]

This second set of misbeliefs, the myth beliefs generating our anxious feelings to begin with, all seem to have the same three-part form or outline. Sometimes our anxious self-talk centers primarily on one or two of these parts, but all of them are there, at least by implication, every time. Here are the three parts of every anxiety misbelief. In place of X, fill in your own irrational fear (e.g., I'll choke; the plane will crash; people will talk about me; whatever):

1. There is a high probability that X will occur.
2. X would be a woeful mishap, a terrible misfortune.
3. To avoid X, I have to glue my attention to it—worry about it, keep myself distressed about it, so it won't happen.

Whether we're mental worriers or physiological reactors, we program ourselves to believe that something ruinous will almost certainly occur, so that we have to concentrate on thinking about it and how dreadful it will be.

Finding Your Own "X"

What is X? That depends on our own private theorizing and learning history. It's always some unwanted event, perceived as ominous, dangerous, deadly, intolerable.

Here's a list you can use to locate some of your own misbeliefs—or perhaps you need to add others:

_____ My dinner for company won't turn out.
_____ The stock market will crash and I'll take a beating.
_____ I know I've upset my boss, and I'll lose my job.

_____ My wife will find out what I've done and divorce me.

_____ What if I get lost in a strange part of town, have to ask directions, and get mugged?

_____ I don't want to go to the doctor, because she might tell me I have a deadly illness.

_____ I don't like to ask people to do things or give me things because they might refuse, and then I'll know for sure they don't really care for me.

_____ I know he'll never ask me out (or she'll never go out with me), and I'll be alone—as always.

_____ We won't have enough to retire on. We'll be destitute.

_____ I could be laid off if the economy gets worse. I'll lose everything.

_____ I might get hurt and be laid up for good.

_____ My son/daughter might be on drugs.

_____ My spouse might be having an affair.

_____ I'm sure _____ doesn't like me.

_____ I'm alienating everyone. Nobody will like me.

_____ The elevator will get stuck between floors, and I'll have trouble breathing.

_____ I'll bore everyone with my speech (music, sermon, etc.), and they'll walk out.

_____ Nobody will want to come to my party, and I'll find out what a social misfit I am.

Add any other of your own anxiety misbeliefs here:

_____

_____

_____

_____

When X Is a Picture: Right-Brain Misbeliefs

I've created these sample X's and presented them in words. But for many people, X is an image, a mental picture. Instead of telling themselves in so many words that they'll have an accident, they see a picture of themselves having a head-on collision on the freeway. They *see* themselves being rejected, being hurt, losing.

Across the movie screen of people with graphic-mode minds, anxiety pictures flash. They may see themselves on the observation deck at the very top of a famed 52-floor building, and suddenly the building tilts. Off they go! Or they see themselves in a closed room, where the air becomes heavy, unbreathable, exhausting. They can almost feel themselves choking, fighting for breath. If only they could open the door before they suffocate!

Persons with dominant right-brain hemispheres may often experience their anxiety self-talk in pictures, while those whose left-brain hemisphere is dominant tend to frighten themselves with words. Whether or not the words come to consciousness, they believe that X, if it happened, would be absolutely cataclysmic for them.

If you experienced problems using the verbal check list above, it could be because you're a visualizer rather than a verbalizer when it comes to X's. If so, run back over the list, turn the words into pictures, and see if any of them correspond to your own.

Finding Your Own Mental Audiovisual

Finding your own anxiety misbeliefs shouldn't be too difficult. Listen with your "inner ear" or look at your private mental movie screen at those times when you're feeling anxious or executing some avoidance maneuver. Write your thoughts out when you're in the midst of anxious feelings. Locate your lies without compromise.

The time to write is when you're most uptight. Why? Because we try to bury our anxiety misbeliefs and forget them, along with the discomfort they evoke.

Once you've found and recorded your own X and the misbeliefs you've been feeding yourself, you're ready to make changes. First, determine whether the probability of X is really high. After all, life does present us with real threats. For instance, how likely is it that the money for the mortgage payment won't be available by the end of the grace period in your contract? If it's really quite likely, then stop wringing your hands and making yourself upset. Instead, start doing something about the situation.

Pray, Then Take Action

Next, get on your knees and pray for God's help, believing that what His Word says is true: He *is* "an ever-present help in trouble" (Psalm 46:1). Then take action. Go ask the lender for an extension, explaining your situation and how you plan to have the money by such-and-such a date. Or consider whether you can sell your new car and drive something a little older, using the difference to make your payment. Whatever else you can do, *do it.*

If you can't do anything except pray, and you have to face the fact that you'll probably lose your house, start planning what you'll do for shelter after that. Then begin to make the arrangements.

Meanwhile, stop telling yourself that you're finished, and that your fate is worse than death. Granted, it's not a happy event to have your home repossessed by the mortgage banker. But it's happened to others before, and they've recovered and gone on with life, with some eventually owning their own homes again.

You don't have to tell yourself it's not painful—it is. But neither do you have to tell yourself it's a disaster. Write out your truthful self-talk right across the page from the disaster-predicting misbeliefs to which it corresponds. Write it in an aggressive, argumentative style. Put up a battle!

Is your X, in fact, very unlikely ever to occur? How probable is it that you really will pass out in church in front of everybody? What's the actual likelihood that you'll catch a terrible disease from touching a doorknob? How sure are you that people will criticize you fiercely for the way you read aloud in Bible class? How many people do you know who have suffocated from trying to breathe in a room with the doors closed? You know that mouse won't attack you or do you any harm even if it does run across your shoe tops.

If the thing you fear is unlikely to happen, you have to change your self-talk and quit predicting it. Write out the truth instead about the real likelihood of X across the page from your predictions.

"Yes," you answer, "but if it *does* happen, it will be so unbearable, so horrible, so awful I can't even let myself think about it!" So now ask yourself seriously: "What if it *did* happen? Exactly what would it be like, what would I do, and what would the outcome be?"

The "Worst Thing" That Could Happen

Except for damnation, isn't death nearly the worst thing that can happen, the bottom line? And none of us can evade death forever, whatever we do. In fact, the most certain item in your future is death!

But Christ Jesus has taken the sting and the victory away from death. The absolute truth is that death—though the timing of it may seem inconvenient and the manner of it may involve discomfort—is a passageway to the eternal bliss that is the inheritance we have through Christ by faith. For the believer, it isn't even *death* anymore, because Christ has abolished death and brought life and immortality to light (see 2 Timothy 1:10).

Even if the thing you fear kills you, it won't devastate you, because what kills your body can't do you any real harm. It can't destroy your soul and therefore it can't destroy *you* (see Matthew 10:28). You may need to write out this truth about death clearly and say it firmly to yourself.

Nevertheless, most of the things you worry about won't kill you, even if they do happen. Most things you expect to be dreadful aren't really dreadful. Most things you've labeled catastrophic aren't really catastrophic. Unpleasant, probably; uncomfortable, yes; difficult, likely. But they won't obliterate you or wipe you out.

Whenever you tell yourself that if it happened you "couldn't stand it," face the fact that you *could* stand it: You could and you would, and you'd probably live through it, too. If this is part of the truth you need to tell yourself, write it out.

"It's So Important for Me to Worry!"

The third part of X—the notion that you must concentrate always on X, worry about it, and never let your mind wander too far from its threat and its horror—makes the least sense of all. After you've taken whatever action you can, then face squarely the fact that there's nothing further you can do to prevent X. And if that's the case, X is in God's hands. Tell yourself the truth about God, His trustworthiness, His perfect love, His faithfulness and constancy, and how even if X kills you, God will keep you and yours in His hand. Ultimately, nothing can harm you, so there's no need to distress yourself over X.

In fact, the more you agitate yourself by repeating to yourself over and over how terrible X is, the worse you'll cope. Once you've given X your best shot by taking sensible precautions, there isn't any improvement in your survival probabilities from getting anxious and "nerved up." Jesus made that very point dramatically with His suggestion that you can't make yourself live a moment longer or grow an inch taller by constantly reminding yourself of X (see Luke 12:25–26 KJV and NIV). Write out this truth to yourself. Tell yourself in no uncertain terms how utterly pointless it is to stew about what may happen.

Getting Truth In

One aspect of growing in faith is to increasingly replace with the truth those falsehoods in your innermost thoughts that you've been hanging on to. So now get the truth into your deepest center, your "inner parts," as David put it in Psalm 51, where he recalls how much God desires just this.

People often ask me "How do I get truth into my heart?" I assume that's your question too if you're getting eager to make war against your own anxieties and worries. In the next chapter we'll discuss six ways by which you can get the truth to flow inside to stoke your faith.

Chapter

13

Moving the Truth Into Your Heart

Dawn has been on my mind lately. She continues to suffer from anxiety in the form of panic attacks. She takes antidepressants faithfully, as prescribed, she's read my books, she understands about the truth, and she reports her self-talk accurately, yet she still endures bouts with panic.

Dawn knows all about the truth, but she still doesn't *know the truth*. Instead, she argues *against* the truth and *for* her perfectionistic, self-condemning misbeliefs. She's like a prosecuting attorney out to get the accused defendant convicted—even though she herself is the accused, and she knows all the facts and arguments proving her innocence.

"I know I'm supposed to accept my faults, but I don't see how I can," she tells me. "For instance, I should be over this problem but I'm not. I'm just not getting any better. I'm not going to get well, am I?"

If I tell her that the great majority of people do get better, she argues that she will surely be one of those who don't improve. If I tell her that her predictions of doom are unfounded and that reiterating them simply makes her worse, she responds that she already realizes that, but she's equally certain that she will keep on making herself worse, no matter how hard she tries to stop. If I tell her that a little anxiety won't do her any harm, she counters that to her my words only mean she'll never be well, that she'll always suffer the way she suffers now. If she reads a book to help herself learn and tell herself the truth, she finds something in the book to focus on that makes her more anxious. If she goes to the

Bible to seek the truth, she only finds how far short of its standards she falls—and gets more depressed and anxious.

Faith Without Confidence

Dawn's grasp of the truth about her anxiety, mostly intellectual, must move from head to heart, from the storage place where her mind stocks up pure information to the place at the core of her soul where self talks to self, the place where self-talk controls feelings and actions.

Maybe you don't know the truth about your anxiety at all, even in your intellect. But it's also possible that you're like Dawn. Perhaps you too "know" the truth about your anxiety with your intellect, but not yet in your heart. With respect to your fears, you may have a kind of faith, but, like the dead faith James describes, it doesn't produce freedom from irrational fears and apprehensions. It is a "faith" without confidence.

Moving the Truth Into Your Heart

If that's the case, you can make use of the following six techniques for moving the truth into your heart:

1. *Pray for the Holy Spirit.* Melinda had consulted me hoping to find a path out of her distressing separation anxiety. Since her very first days at school, having to be away from her mother, and later, from her home, had been difficult and at times impossible. Now, at thirty-three, Melinda had great difficulty forcing herself to take any trip outside of her own city.

We worked for a while on identifying Melinda's misbeliefs. She found them and she learned the truth that ought to replace them—by rote. But nothing changed. Melinda was still afraid and, more significantly, she continued dosing herself with her old misbeliefs.

What was wrong? What could make a difference? To answer those questions, we went through the Scriptures to examine the role of the Holy Spirit.

The Holy Spirit does many things for God's children. But with Melinda

I wanted to zero in on His role as the One who can graft the truth into our heart. Jesus named Him the "Spirit of truth," and promised that He would guide us into all the truth (see John 16:13). We all understand that Jesus was not promising the Holy Spirit would engrave the entire Encyclopedia Britannica on the hearts of believers, but rather He was referring to the truth of His own teachings, including His teaching that His people don't need to live in anxiety and fear (see Matthew 6:25-34).

This was precisely the truth we wanted for Melinda. So we prayed for the Holy Spirit, keeping in mind Jesus' own special promise covering such prayers, guaranteeing that God *will* "give the Holy Spirit to those who ask him!" (Luke 11:1-13). Here is the prayer we used:

> *Enlighten my mind, O God, by your Holy Spirit, who comes forth from You, that, as your Son Jesus has promised, I may be led into all truth; in the name of Jesus Christ, my Lord. Amen.*

In addition, Melinda learned to pray for the Spirit of truth "in the crunch"—right at those precise times when she had to do something that likely would make her anxious.

Many people like Melinda have prayed for the Holy Spirit in my office. Sometimes they experience nothing at that moment; sometimes the client senses great peace within; occasionally what appears to be a complete cure occurs. But always this prayer establishes a factual basis for believing the divine promise that the power of the truth will be at work within the person battling anxiety.

2. *Immerse yourself in the Scriptures.* It's my impression that many Christians read the Bible or believe they ought to read the Bible as a kind of obligation, a sacred duty, like honoring parents, giving money, going to church, or praying. I think this notion is deadly because it obscures the real reasons for soaking up Scripture like a sponge. The *real* reasons are not that it's something you "must" do or "ought" to do

because God "commands" it. In fact, it's not easy to find in the Bible any direct command to read the Bible!

Actually, I believe the two major reasons for immersing yourself in the Scriptures are these: First, the Bible is the source of all final and absolute truth, the only truth on which you can certainly count. Second, the Word is one of the means through which the Holy Spirit works changes in the hearts (or self-talk centers) of believers, changes that amount to potent and effective faith.

That is, the Word of God is not only flawlessly correct, but it is also *powerful* because the Holy Spirit comes to us, enters our hearts, and works in us through it. So the Word is not only like a measuring stick for determining truth, it's like food and water energizing the person who wants to walk in truth.[1] Eat and drink from the Scriptures because you need their divine power working the truth into your heart, not just into your head. Feed on the Word, because by it the Holy Spirit implants the truth into the garden of your soul's center.

3. *Expose yourself, by experience, to the truth at work.* Let yourself actually experience contact with the thing you fear irrationally. It's on this very step that Dawn and I are working now. This is the step we've discussed previously in slightly different terms, calling it *exposure* and *response prevention*.

In this step you begin, in some way large or small, to defy your old avoidance habit patterns. In Dawn's case, we're doing it by having her visualize frightening situations while she's deeply relaxed. In others, we plan that the client will jump right into the full force of the situation and simply take all the anxiety until it wears out. And in still others, the client plans to expose him or herself gradually to increasingly saturated doses of the feared situation.

The point is to discover in actual experience that the feared situation doesn't do any damage to you and that the anxiety itself will finally diminish or even dissipate completely. Experience—direct encounter with real situations and their effect on you—can change a fact you know only in your head to a life-changing belief implanted firmly in your heart.

4. *Expose yourself to the experiences of others.* We need to share the

experiences of other Christians, through their conversations and sometimes directly. That's one reason why we need the Christian fellowship
of the church. Vicarious experience, though not as powerful as our own
encounters with reality, can markedly reduce anxiety by moving truth
from head to heart.

Laura had developed a mighty fear of nearly everything that she
believed could contain ground glass. She feared that she might acci-
dentally swallow ground glass and die. She began avoiding sugar, salt,
restaurant food, and flour because—who knew?—they could contain
ground glass and she'd never find it.

Now it's important to tell you that Laura knew in her intellect that
the probability of any of this happening was so exceedingly low as to be
negligible. But she didn't know it in her heart. So I asked her to bring
some ground glass to her next treatment session.

She brought some in a small metal box. I promptly immersed my
hands in the stuff, poured it from one hand to the other, rubbed my
hands on my skin, on my face, and even on my lips. She watched in
horrified fascination. But as I continued handling the glass with no ill
effects, Laura became willing to touch it, then to imitate my actions.

Eventually, she lost her fear that every substance she encountered
might be full of ground glass. By watching my experience, her belief
that ground glass wasn't so terrible began moving from head to heart
and she was able to go ahead and get well.

Most people have had the experience of daring to do something that
was frightening to them, after they watched someone they trusted do it
without harmful effects: jumping off the high board; getting on the horse
that seemed so large and dangerous; climbing through a broken window
into a deserted old warehouse. Now, in the same way, watching others
do what frightens us and letting them be our models can be the starting
point to begin countering our anxiety misbeliefs in the heart, for bringing
our faith in the truth down from the intellect into the life center.

5. *Learn to argue effectively.* Learn to argue for the truth! This may
appear to be a strange bit of advice, contrary to what you've been led

to believe. When you think of argument, you may picture people acting angry, aggressive, and impolite. But in fact, argument need not involve quarreling or fighting! Argument can be positive, loving, and cheerful. And argument is one of the best skills you can master for becoming deeply convinced of the truth.

Four hundred years before Christ, a wise and good man named Socrates sought the truth in the marketplace of Athens. Socrates led men gently into the truth by argument (often called dialogue). True, he never argued with intent to wound or humiliate another person, nor did Socrates argue to exalt himself. His goal was to discover and live by the truth and to help others do the same.

Some therapists argue with their clients (I do, sometimes with pretty good results!) to help them become so convinced of the truth that it will take hold in their hearts. If you have that kind of therapist, he or she will expect you to debate and defend your misbeliefs while he or she argues to defeat them. As you engage in argument with the therapist, you'll probably imitate and assimilate the therapist's strategies. Later, you can use the same tactics to argue down your own misbeliefs, making room in your heart for the truth to take root and grow.

Here's an example of what I mean by therapeutic argument:

"I'm sure God has left me."
"Why are you so sure?"
"Because I don't feel His presence."
"How did you feel when you felt His presence?"
"Good."
"You mean that now you don't feel good?"
"Right. I feel terrible."
"And your not feeling good demonstrates the absence of God?"
"I guess that's what I'm saying."
"How did Jesus feel when He was weeping over Jerusalem?"
"Not very good, I guess."
"Was God absent from Him?"
"No. He was always close to God."

"How did Abraham feel when he was binding his son, Isaac, to a sacrificial altar?"

"Pretty bad, I guess."

"Was God absent?"

"No. He was there. He stopped the sacrifice of Isaac."

"Do you still think your feeling bad proves that God is absent?"

"I guess it can't prove God is absent, can it?"

Or consider another example:

"I can't stand any more of those terrible feelings!"

"You can't stand the feelings?"

"No, I can't stand them anymore!"

"What will you do if they occur again?"

"I don't know. I don't want them anymore! I can't take them!"

"You can't stand them and you can't take them anymore, but you don't know what you'll do if they occur again?"

"No."

"I know what you'll do."

"What?"

"You'll stand them and take them. What else is there to do? And you'll get through them, too, just as you have before."

"Yes, I guess I will."

Instead of defending your own misbeliefs against the arguments and reasoning of a counselor, try reversing the process. Tangle in spirited argument with the misbeliefs of your friend. When it's appropriate, if someone you know asks for help or advice, turn the process around.

Let's say someone you know tells you about his own anxiety, making it obvious that she needs and wants your help and advice. Now *you* are the counselor. Don't hesitate! God brought His people together in order that, among other services, they might teach and admonish one another.

Your friend tells you her anxiety is so bad she can't stand it. You'll now argue, gently, persuasively, asking questions like Socrates did and like the counselor in the example above. Keep asking until your friend admits that she was overstating things when she said, "I can't stand this!" and instead agrees that she *can* stand her anxiety, though she would much rather not. That, as you know, is the truth.

From there you might move on to other anxiety misbeliefs. The important thing is that here your role is to argue *for the truth* and *against the misbeliefs* that are destroying your friend's peace of mind. This is a service of love, but you'll also benefit yourself, because in arguing with someone else's misbeliefs, you are massaging the truth deeper into your own heart.

You might find it profitable to study some of *Plato's Dialogues of Socrates*[2] to see for yourself how Socrates could bring the other person ever so considerately to discover and acknowledge the truth. Imitating some of his methods of argument can be helpful.

Finally, your major life-and-death arguments must be with yourself, against your own misbeliefs. If you're alive in Christ Jesus, filled with the Holy Spirit of truth, you carry with you a situation ripe for argument! For the new person you are in Christ Jesus repeatedly has to take issue with the person you were, the old *you* allied with the devil, the world, and the sinful flesh. The sinfulness that can still cling to the person who has been crucified with Christ Jesus and raised by the Father to new life. That sinful flesh, which once was *you*, will try to foster the devil's old lies in your mind to make you ever more anxious.

The arguments in this situation will be similar to the arguments between your misbeliefs and your counselor-therapist and between you and the fleshly misbeliefs of your friend. Only now you'll argue with your own old nature, the sinful flesh, which still hangs around trying to make trouble even though you're now dead to it in Christ. These arguments may not always be so kind.

Paul refers to another battle in Ephesians 6:10–18, the battle against the forces of darkness. Fighting this war gives you practical experience in the sort of believing faith that can quench all the fiery darts of unbelief and misbelief in the arsenal of your three enemies: the devil, the world, and the flesh.

Here's a sample dialogue between you and the old you—that is, between the new person and the sinful, lying flesh:

- *Your flesh:* "Nobody will be your friend or like you since you blew your speech because of your anxiety."
- *You:* "What about God? Does He dislike, reject, and desert people who get anxious?"
- *Flesh:* "I guess not. I guess He loves everybody. So what?"
- *You:* "So this: If God hasn't left me, I don't have to be afraid of people because He's the best friend a person can have and the only friend I absolutely need. In fact, I'll get over my anxiety a lot quicker if I face the fact that while it's nice to have human beings like and admire me, it's not critical. It's critical for me to be at one with God! And that's where I am through Christ Jesus, who gave everything for me."
- *Flesh:* "All that religious stuff sounds fine, but it doesn't change the fact that you screwed up again, and that being anxious is a terrible social liability. Life is a disaster when people don't like you."
- *You:* "People dislike those they perceive as anxious?"
- *Flesh:* "Most people admire those who are cool, strong, and competent, not those who are nervous and tense."
- *You:* "You said 'admire.' Is that the same as 'like'?"
- *Flesh:* "No. But when you're nervous and anxious, people won't *like* you either!"
- *You:* "I wonder if that's so. I like Ellen, and she won't even try to get up and make a speech. She goes into a panic if you even mention anything like that to her. And when I see somebody who's nervous when they're making a speech, I feel close to them, not like I want to reject them. Especially if they start right off

and admit they're nervous. I admire their frankness. I think this notion of yours is dead wrong!"

- *Flesh:* "Just wait till the next speech you have to make. You'll make a real fool of yourself, in spite of all these fine ideas!"
- *You:* "Maybe so, and maybe not. But I won't avoid it. Instead, I'll pray about it and think about how I can get along without human approval if I have to, so long as God loves me. And I'll rethink the old misbelief that people will dislike me if they know I'm anxious. I think you've been lying to me!"

6. *Cultivate new habits.* Develop new mental habits by practicing and practicing and more practicing. Develop the habit of noticing what's going on in your thinking when you're avoiding something out of fear or when you're feeling anxious. Most people pay attention to events outside their own skins and to feelings and events in their bodies—while they ignore the thoughts that are producing their anxious feelings and avoidance-oriented actions. Practice treating anxious feelings as signals alerting you to ask yourself: *"What am I telling myself right now? What am I believing and thinking? How are these thoughts creating anxiety?"*

Develop the mental habit of taking issue with and arguing against untruth in your own mind. ("That notion certainly is painful and threatening. Is it really so? Let me look at it again.") Learn to go on and ask yourself in what way these anxiety-generating thoughts are untruthful, contrary to fact, or needlessly threatening. ("If it happened, would I survive? Would it be as bad as I'm telling myself it would be? Or would it only be unpleasant?")

Develop the mental habit of searching out the truth and then practice substituting the truth for the untruthful and threatening thoughts you find. ("I have to admit, getting dizzy and lightheaded, sweating, having a rapid heartbeat, and so on, are *not* dangerous like I've been assuming. They're normal signs of anxiety. That's all.")

Practice arguing against your erroneous beliefs until arguing becomes a habit, a good habit, a habit of faith.

Accepting Anxious Feelings

I had never seen anyone like Alex until yesterday. A new client, he brought two complaints. First he suffered from a most unpleasant disease that had been pronounced incurable, nonfatal, and "undiagnosable" by medical experts. A second part of his struggle was a sudden drop in income related to his illness.

"But why have you consulted a *clinical psychologist?*" I queried, puzzled. "Support? Stress reduction? Your physicians at Mayo haven't suggested your illness is *psychological.* Your sagging income isn't an emotional disorder either. These are aggravations, not a mental illness you can recover from by talking to me! You're dealing with some unpleasant *facts,* not delusions!"

"*I don't like facts!*" Alex screamed back at me. "*I don't want to adjust!*"

Though I was correct—and it was inappropriate to give him psychological treatment for an organic illness or a drop in income—I had irritated him greatly. What I wanted him to aim at was acceptance. I would like to have helped him accept facts and live with them contentedly. But he rejected such a goal and left my office a very dissatisfied customer.

Anxiety: A Given!

We don't have to be like Alex and just walk out on reality. Instead, we can take to heart what I said to Alex about accepting facts. Anxiety, sometimes intense anxiety, is a fact of life. Those who want to get over crippling anxiety can and will improve. They probably won't get anxiety entirely out of their lives, but they need not be debilitated.

Are you nervous when you have to confront somebody? Join the crowd! Are you tense, uncomfortable when you're asked to give your testimony in church? You're not alone! Does interviewing for a job give you butterflies and sweaty palms? The more you try to cover up your fidgets the more you stammer, stutter, and generally blow it? You're not overly thrilled when you have to turn down a request? Taking tests puts you on edge? Are you a little jittery when you look down from the balcony of your twentieth floor hotel room? Yes! You and nine-tenths of the human race share at least some of these experiences.

Life is full of annoyances, irritations, vexations, to-do's, and crises. Normal human life contains some anxiety; after all, it's a struggle—described in the Bible as a *battle*.[1] No Scripture passage refers to life as a pain in the neck, but that's what it often is.

Many people like Alex have erroneously concluded that the Christian faith, when everything is working properly, should guarantee that they'll never have an incurable disease or a shortage of funds. They think they've been told that God surely wants them rich and famous. They're determined to get "vic'try all the time" and mean by this that their lives had better be free from nuisances—or else.

But that's not the picture of life painted by the Holy Spirit on the canvas of Scripture. Nor is it the view we get when we survey human history. Instead, we learn from Scripture and experience that nobody can go through life without sickness, without the loss of loved ones, rejection, criticism, mistakes, times of utter loneliness, physical pain, and emotional anguish. There's seldom enough money for everything; most children occasionally disappoint their parents; spouses don't live up to rosy premarital expectations; and our team doesn't always win the Super Bowl.

The English novelist Thomas Hardy observed that nothing, in reality, ever meets our expectation. And I would add that nothing is ever so good that there's no room for even a smidgen of anxiety around the edges!

Major Misbelief: I Shouldn't Have Any Pain

Many people like Alex hate to be reminded of reality. They reject its existence even while they're enmeshed in it and try to convince themselves that they must be able to get through life without pain if only they have enough "faith" (which they take to mean something like a high-decibel "spirituality"). Some people even take it to mean they're shoddy Christians if they experience any misery from anxiety! They're sure there's something dreadfully wrong with their relationship with Christ.

What I'm trying to say is that some anxiety, like death and taxes, is a fact of life. It isn't the purpose of Christian faith, or for that matter of honest psychology, to enable you to float languidly above the fray. Alex needed to accept his limitations no matter how vehemently he insisted that they go away. And you too must learn to accept anxious feelings as part of your human existence. You can get better, but you probably can't get totally "over it" because anxiety isn't a disease. It's a normal human emotion, part of life on this side of the resurrection.

It's not only a part of human life. A few minutes before savage bolts of Minnesota lightning pound into our dreams during summer nights, our bed begins to shake. The cause is Mocha's tremors. Our 160-pound German shepherd will have heard the approaching storm and huddled as close against our bed frame as she can possibly squeeze, while her petrified panting assails our ears and the bed vibrates violently with her shivering.

We can't know without interviewing her exactly what Mocha feels inside. But her behavioral signs during thunderstorms closely resemble acute human anxiety! Apparently, anxiety is part of life even for normal, healthy dogs.

We've pointed out before that Jesus himself experienced violent emotion on the night of His arrest, sweating beads of perspiration "like great drops of blood." We're lacking any report of what He felt inside. But the context and description given in the Gospels make it reasonable to conclude that the God-Man, was, at least once or twice, wrenched by anxiety.

Even Anxiety Experts Get Anxious

Even those people you'd vow should never feel the slightest fear get anxious under the right circumstances. Indeed, experts on anxiety get anxious! David Burns, a professor of psychiatry and a leading authority on anxiety, has written engagingly about his own nervous fears in various social situations, telling of experiences nearly everyone can identify with, including his miserable embarrassment while presenting a talk to fellow professionals.[2] The anxiety experts have to face anxiety too.

Amazing for their low levels of anxiety are those risk-taking, consequence-ignoring thrill-seekers whom psychologists label *antisocial personalities*. Max came to our attention in the hospital where he'd been brought raving drunk by the police. It was probably not the place for him, but Max had a way of getting off easy.

We had seen Max several times in the same condition. Somehow he always managed to sober up and talk his way out of trouble. But if you sat down and read his record, you'd find it incredible that he hadn't been locked up in the penitentiary for life!

Notable for his pursuit of dangerous excitement and risky thrills, Max had also taken incredible chances in his brushes with the law. He appeared fearless—so cool everyone he knew would have vowed he never felt anxious—until he was locked up in the psychiatry ward. Then Max, the quintessential sociopathic personality, would pace nervously up and down the ward, complaining of anxious distress, begging for tranquilizers.

Even seemingly nerveless sociopaths who might hold up a bank without a tremor can become anxious when they're confined in a ward or in a prison cell (where many of them actually spend the balance of their lives). Anxiety occasionally catches up with sociopaths too.

I realize some of my readers will not enjoy this chapter. Some people hate and fear their anxiety with inordinate fervor, and they don't want to hear about anxiety as a part of life! How about you? Do you find yourself resenting the message that you can't have a life without anxiety?

Hating Anxiety Creates Anxiety

I don't blame you for not getting a big kick out of the news that you can't escape anxiety entirely. But in a world where dogs, anxiety experts, sociopaths, and even the Son of God have faced it, you won't rid your life of it by hating it and refusing to face it!

In fact, you can fear and hate anxiety so much you actually make it worse. Some people wind themselves up into a ball of tension trying to avoid every scrap of it. Like Alex, they say they don't like facts, and they want someone to remove the facts for them. But by reacting so intensely against even the idea of anxiety, they generate more of the very tension and fearfulness from which they wish so ardently to escape.

Tune in on their self-talk: "I can't ever go through that again," they tell themselves after experiencing a robust round of anxious reactions and feelings. "It was too terrible! I have to make sure it doesn't hit me anymore." They move on from irrational fear of events in the environment to creating their own fear of fear itself.

What they suffer from, then, is the anxiety they've created by unrealistically demanding total freedom from the anxieties of life. Then they go on to plan how they'll avoid whatever might make them even a little bit anxious. We've already seen what faith does with that.

We Don't Mind Strong Doses of Joy!

Why is it so difficult to learn to accept anxiety? We usually accept other strong emotions without too much difficulty. You don't find people going to a therapist to get rid of their *joy* because it's so overwhelming!

Occasionally I see patients who request help controlling their anger because other people have served notice that they won't put up with their outbursts. But I can't recall any of my clients saying, "I need to get rid of my anger because I can't stand the terrible, intense feelings!" Sometimes people will want help controlling feelings of illicit attraction because these feelings have gotten them into trouble. But nobody says, "Take these powerful feelings of attraction away—I can't stand them."

Misbeliefs About Anxiety

So why do we fear feelings of anxiety so? Like joy, anger, and love, they're nothing more than our own feelings. Sometimes anxious feelings are generated by nothing at all in the environment, but by misbeliefs *about anxiety itself!*

Here are some of the most common misbeliefs about anxiety held by people who worry about the possibility that they will get anxious:

- "Anxiety is unnatural and shouldn't be happening."
- "Anxiety is all right for other people, but it shouldn't happen to me because I'm a believer."
- "Anxiety is extremely bad for me because it's so stressful."
- "Anxiety causes death."
- "If I get anxious enough I might lose control."
- "If people see my anxiety they'll think I'm weird."
- "Others will reject me if they know I'm anxious."
- "It's of crucial importance to get rid of anxiety *now!*"
- "I'll probably cause an accident if I get anxious when I'm driving."
- "Others don't feel this way, so they won't understand."

Trying to Avoid Anxiety Can Cause Anxiety

As you read the preceding list of misbeliefs, say them aloud to yourself and pay attention to any feelings they may evoke. Surprised? Feel the butterflies? The tense muscles? The more conviction you can work up as you repeat these misbeliefs to yourself, the more intensely you will also feel them.

Now, the point: If you really believe such notions and lard your internal speech with them day after day, you can be certain you'll increase your tension, wind yourself up into a tight ball, and maintain a state of anxiety—even *though you're trying to avoid and prevent anxious feelings.* So you confront the anxiety paradox: The more you try to overcome anxiety by thinking about how bad it is, the more anxious you make yourself.

The Solution: Accept Your Anxiety

The solution then, in part anyway, is to accept anxiety if you feel it. Ask yourself, "What am I telling myself now that is making me feel so uptight? And what am I trying to accomplish by tensing myself up like this? I'm going to relax. And I'll examine my self-talk (or the mental images I'm picturing). I'll stop telling myself I have to get rid of this anxiety at all costs, and instead, I'll take what comes, relax, and get into the truth by faith!"

Reinterpret your anxious feelings truthfully. Instead of telling yourself erroneously how anxiety is injurious, tell yourself anxious feelings are only your own feelings, generated by your body, which is operating just as it should in response to what your mind feeds it. You don't have to control these feelings, and nothing terrible will happen to you if you don't, even if your anxious feelings become very strong. Your body is doing many of the same things it would do if you had just run a couple of miles.

THE GOOD NEWS ABOUT WORRY

The Truth

Study carefully what Aaron Beck, Gary Emery, and Ruth Greenberg, three of the world's leading authorities on anxiety disorders, suggest that you tell yourself:

> *There is literally nothing else that you can be aware of but feelings and sensations. If you're afraid of making a fool of yourself when giving a speech, what you're really afraid of are your sensations of anxiety, self-consciousness, and shame. And if you're afraid of dying in an accident, you're actually afraid of the inferred sensation and panic of being out of control, as well as of the anticipated pain of the injury.* By accepting these feelings, you can lessen them. *(emphasis added)*[3]

These experts add to this insight a quotation from H. L. Weinberg:

> *Knowing that the only thing we can really fear is ourselves, the only fear is fear of ourselves, of pain (which is something our own tissues generate) of some kind, and this pain through acceptance becomes endurable, helps breed a quiet courage and sensible serenity which in turn prevents many psychosomatic ills from developing in the future.*[4]

Weinberg said this well. But the apostle Paul, inspired by the Holy Spirit and writing specifically to Christians, whose faith empowers them to endure, described even more radiantly the advantage of accepting and enduring painful feelings, including feelings of anxiety:

> *We also rejoice in our sufferings, because we know that suffering produces perseverance; perseverance, character; and character, hope. And hope does not disappoint us, because God has poured out his love into our hearts by the Holy Spirit, whom he has given us. (Romans 5:3–5)*

You who are terrified of your own anxious feelings, pay attention! All you can possibly be fearful of are your own feelings. Instead of scaring the wits out of yourself about your feelings, tell yourself what they are: nothing but your own feelings!

Tell yourself that they exist whether you like them or not. They may not be very comfortable, but you won't start plastering hideous labels on them ("dangerous," "wrong," "terrible," "signs of impending doom and catastrophe about to happen"). Rather, tell yourself you'll accept them for what they are and no more than that.

Tell yourself, "I don't have to enjoy them, but I don't have to keep on panicking and trying to run from them. If I just bear them, I'll get through them and they'll go away eventually. They'll not do me any harm. In fact, by faith, God can use them to work endurance, character, and true hope in me through Jesus Christ!"

A Continual Dialogue With the *Flesh*

Finally, remember that the moment you begin to accept anxious feelings instead of trying your level best to escape and avoid them—*that very moment*, you can be rid of the top layer of tension that you've brought on yourself by believing it's imperative to get rid of your own anxious feelings. And at that very moment, you've come a long, long way toward wholeness!

Lessening Phobic Anxiety

Fortune had smiled on Marc. He owned a car dealership with the local franchise for the make and model everybody wanted. But now Marc was up against it. He'd had a simple accident.

At first the other guy had admitted being at fault. But now he'd changed his mind. His insurance company had decided to contest Marc's claim, and the courtroom was on the ninth floor of the county courthouse.

Marc was panic-stricken. Heights terrified him. The third floor of any building was his limit!

As soon as he heard where the hearing would take place, terrifying images crowded through Marc's mind. He saw himself crouching in court, getting so tense he couldn't sit still, losing control, and making a fool of himself. He saw the astonished judge ordering him locked up in a state facility with bars on the windows. He knew he needed help.

Marc had heard I performed what was then a new treatment for phobic anxiety called *systematic desensitization*, developed by Dr. Joseph Wolpe, a behavioral psychiatrist. Marc came to see if I thought the treatment would help him. I explained how avoidance had kept his fear of heights alive, and how exposure to high places would be necessary to reverse the fear.[1]

Marc immediately rejected the idea of going to the highest floor at the center and sweating it out the way Rick had done (see chapter 10). He thought such raw immersion in anxiety would be too traumatic for him. Instead, he chose systematic desensitization. We set to work immediately, and by the time the court hearing occurred a few weeks later, he astonished himself by sitting calmly in the courtroom without distress.

Maybe the Greeks Were On to Something

The ancient Greeks made fear a god and named it *Phobos*. Our word *phobia* comes from the name of this dread-provoking deity. Maybe those Greeks of long ago understood something profound about human psychology and spirituality: By submitting so totally to our fears that we let them determine our actions, we turn them into little gods in place of the true God.

Strictly speaking, a *phobia* is a specific, persistent, irrational fear of something of which the sufferer is well aware. So if you feel a nameless dread no matter what situation you're in, your fear isn't a phobia because you don't know what you're afraid of and can't very well avoid it. If you're afraid of playing catch with a loaded gun, your fear isn't a phobia because it's rational and the danger is real. People with phobias usually know precisely what they fear and plan their lives in such a way as to avoid the objects of their fears.

Here are some examples of phobias and their fancy "official" names:

ophidiophobia: fear of snakes
acrophobia: fear of heights
hydrophobia: fear of water
astraphobia: fear of lightning
brontophobia: fear of thunder

Almost anything can become an object of phobic anxiety, although certain things are more commonly feared than others. Flying, blood, open wounds, public speaking, dentists, test-taking, being alone, the police, dogs, darkness, hospitals, spiders, cats, bugs, germs, radiation exposure, consumption of chocolate, doctors, closed spaces—almost any object or situation can play a part in a phobia.

We should keep in mind that although the definition of *phobia* is correct, it might be a bit arbitrary. Often, people who are diagnosed as having generalized anxiety rather than a phobia are actually quite aware of some of their fears. The perfectionist fears being evaluated, making a mistake, or doing something less than flawlessly, and very often knows exactly what he or she fears. Sometimes, a generalized anxiety disorder really amounts to a fear of other people's opinions or negative evaluations, a fear of which the victim is usually well aware. So what we have to say about phobias may be applicable to many other irrational anxieties as well.

Spiritual Roots of Phobic Anxiety

How can a phobia be a problem with spiritual roots? Phobias are not presented that way in the clinical textbooks. Yet nearly every person who has come to faith has discovered that having a rich spiritual life does impart courage and strength to replace anxieties and fears. And vital, living faith will work within phobia victims a desire to overcome anxieties.

The phobic person controls the anxiety by his or her own devices—specifically by avoidance—rather than by trust, faith, and performance of responsibility. In some ways phobias are often easy to live with because phobics have their anxiety wrapped up in a single fear so all they have to do to remain comfortable is stay away from the feared object. Stay out of elevators and your elevator phobia won't bother you. Keep yourself away from balconies and your height phobia won't hurt much. Tell your friends you're allergic to cats (when you're really afraid of them) and they'll keep their pet felines out of the room when you're visiting.

But this kind of success is a deception. Avoidance preserves fear, which increases avoidance, which in turn preserves and increases fear.

So meanwhile you may be planning your life around your fears, avoiding what you fear along with what your faith knows is your responsibility.

When faith comes along, it motivates you to do what you've been avoiding. Faith will guide you to do what God has called you to do. Moreover, faith will create a *desire* to do what you ought to do. So faith may put an end to the comfort afforded by avoidance. But if you give it a chance, it will in place of comfort give you confidence, as much as is necessary to move ahead into what you fear.

How to Conquer Phobic Fears

What can you do to conquer a phobia? First, recognize why it's worthwhile to get over the fear. Often, people with phobias are so successful at planning their lives around avoidance that they lose sight of the concessions they've made to their fears. Avoidance has become so nearly automatic that they don't even notice the callings of God they shy away from or the distortions of the truth they palm off on themselves and others just because of their fears.

The cost of fear is high. A conviction that anxiety is dreadful and that you shouldn't have to experience any might seem like an innocent fiction, but it's not. That fiction prevents your considering how to get over the phobia. After all, you can stay comfortable by avoidance. So let your faith convince you: Phobic anxiety is worth conquering in faith!

Second, understand the misbeliefs underpinning your anxiety and avoidance. Do you believe you shouldn't ever have to be uncomfortable? That you *must never* feel anxiety? Do you tell yourself it's up to you to protect yourself against exposure to things that make you very uncomfortable?

Does your lifestyle actually proclaim the vicious fiction that phobic anxiety is a little god that should set the terms by which you will conduct your daily affairs? Do you practice a kind of self-salvation by avoidance?

It's time for you to stop and think about these matters. Ask yourself what you tell yourself about preserving your phobia. Write down the self-talk that occurs when you shut your eyes, and imagine deliberately encountering what your phobia keeps you away from now.

Third, understand the genuine security you have by faith. It's not the fictitious security you buy yourself at the price of avoidance, but a security which frees you to follow where the Spirit of truth leads. The security of faith says: "Stop avoidance, stop missing out on God's good gifts, stop ducking your responsibilities. Instead, venture forth in response to God's calling wherever it takes you, even if it means you must expose yourself to the things you fear. Your reward will be recovery and freedom!"

Exposure

Sometimes it's just not practical to expose yourself head-on to the things you fear. For instance, if you could get on a plane every day and fly until your upset feelings peter out, no doubt you would soon recover from your fear of flying. But putting such a plan into effect might simply cost more than you can afford.

Moreover, most people, given a choice, strongly prefer not to encounter their fears directly and all at once.[2] They would rather face their fears gradually in small doses.

That was the way Marc wanted to work. So we began with deep relaxation training, and at the same time we began creating a graded series of scenes in which Marc would later imagine himself participating. These scenes would expose him to the bugaboo that made him anxious: higher floors in tall buildings.

Here is Marc's *hierarchy*—the technical name for the list of scenes given in order from the easiest to the most difficult:

1. Walking to the front door of a twenty-story building.
2. Entering the twenty-story building on the ground floor.
3. Standing at the elevator, looking at a list of offices and various floors.

4. Pushing the elevator call button.

5. Entering the elevator and holding it on the ground floor.

6. Riding to the second floor.

7. Entering an office on the second floor and sitting in a waiting room.

8. Riding to the third floor.

9. Entering an office on the third floor and sitting in a waiting room.

10. Riding to the fourth floor.

11. Entering an office on the fourth floor and sitting in a waiting room.

12. Looking out the window on the fourth floor.

13. Entering an office on the sixth floor and sitting in a waiting area.

14.-20. Scenes of remaining on various floors and looking out windows, up to twenty stories.

If you believe desensitization would be appropriate for your anxiety you'd do well to consider professional treatment from a clinical psychologist or counselor using this method. If for any reason professional help is unavailable to you, you can desensitize yourself by creating your own hierarchy, practicing deep relaxation (see chapter 9), and imagining yourself living through the scenes in your hierarchy one at a time while you're profoundly relaxed. Here's what to do:

1. Determine the "theme" of your anxiety hierarchy. Sometimes more than one theme occurs in your scenes. For instance, you might have some anxiety scenes in which you're talking to strangers and others having to do with flying in airplanes. These are separate themes, so you'll have to deal with one of them at a time, constructing separate hierarchies for each.

2. For each hierarchy, think of a series of ten to twenty scenes representing situations that would make you anxious. For each

scene, provide a number from 1 to 100 signifying how much anxiety you would feel in that situation. Your scenes should be between 1 and 10 units apart in their "anxiety ratings," and should range from very low (about 5 or 10 units) to the worst you can imagine (about 95 to 100).

3. Teach yourself deep relaxation and practice it until you feel deeply relaxed.

4. Relax profoundly, and while relaxed imagine the first scene on your hierarchy. Visualize the details, see the colors, the shapes, the persons or things in the scene: Imagine hearing the sounds, smelling the odors, feeling the sensations, doing the actions. Keep the scene in mind for thirty to sixty seconds or until you feel anxiety aroused by it.

5. If you feel anxious at any time, stop picturing the scene and attend to any tension in your muscles. Canvass all your muscle groups mentally and relax any areas of tension. Then return to the scene you left and imagine it until you have done so without anxiety for thirty to sixty seconds. If you feel anxious again, repeat this step.

6. When you have managed to visualize a scene without anxiety, move on up your hierarchy to the next level of difficulty. If your eyes are closed, you may open them to read the next scene—or you may be able to remember the scenes you want to work on during a session.

7. Repeat the process described for each scene. You might try to get through two or three scenes in a session. Work on your hierarchy daily until you can imagine all the scenes without anxiety. This might take several days to several weeks. Continue to practice deep relaxation and learn to relax more and more deeply as you go on with your work.

Here's one more sample hierarchy to illustrate the approach. It's one most people may be able to use since it deals with a commonly encountered anxiety-arousing situation: speaking in public. I'll present a list of scenes having to do with giving a presentation in church.

1. Someone is asking you to give a brief talk three Sundays from now.

2. You are agreeing to present a short talk in three weeks.

3. You are outlining a short talk to be given two and a half weeks from now.

4. You are writing a short talk to be given two weeks from now.

5. You are reading your short talk over aloud—to be given in one week.

6. You are in church listening to someone else give a talk in the same series as yours. Your own talk is a week away.

7. In front of a mirror you are reading your talk aloud—to be given in one week.

8. You are reading your talk aloud to a family member or friend—to be given in one week.

9. You are delivering your talk aloud to two or three family members.

10. You are delivering your talk aloud to two or three strangers.

11. You are delivering your talk aloud to five or ten strangers.

12. You are delivering your talk aloud to fifteen or twenty people, both friends and strangers.

13. You are delivering your talk in church to about fifty people.

14. You are delivering your talk in church to about a hundred people.

15. You are delivering your talk to the entire congregation.

Direct-Exposure Desensitization

Some fears are such that you can expose yourself to them directly. If the mere suggestion stirs up the butterflies in your stomach, calm down. Don't worry: Even direct exposure can be done gradually.

Maybe we should call this *reality desensitization*. Instead of exposing yourself to the things that make you anxious in fantasy, you may want to try gradual and systematic desensitization *in vivo* (in the life situation), as clinicians describe it. Here you also construct a hierarchy, but for *in vivo* desensitization you construct a hierarchy for the purpose of actually doing it.

Suppose, for example, you fear and avoid cats, but your new roommate wants to have a cat and you think it's about time you got over this small drag on your life. You can make a hierarchy, exposing yourself very gradually to small doses of "cat."

Here's an example:

1. You're looking through a picture book about cats.
2. You're going with your friend to a pet store and looking at kittens in the window.
3. You're going with your friend into a pet store, remaining fifteen or twenty feet from the kittens in the window.
4. Your friend is holding a small kitten in another room while you sit in the living room of your apartment.
5. Your friend is holding the kitten in the same room with you, but ten feet away.
6. Same as No. 5, but five feet away.
7. Same as 5, but three feet away.
8. Same as 5, but about a foot from you.
9. You touch the kitten on its back and withdraw your fingers immediately.
10. Same as No. 9, but you touch the kitten for three seconds.
11. Same as 9, but you touch for ten seconds.
12. Same as 9, but you touch for sixty seconds.
13. You pet the kitten with one hand and then both hands as your friend holds it.
14. You hold the kitten for ten seconds.
15. You hold the kitten for thirty seconds.

16. You hold the kitten for one minute.

17. You hold the kitten for ten minutes or longer.

18.–32. You repeat scenes 4–17, but this time you graduate to holding an adult cat.

What Do Phobics Tell Themselves?

We've already seen how changing our self-talk can make us willing to face our fears, for example, in desensitization. But it works the other way too. Desensitization can change our self-talk.

If you try it, you'll discover for yourself that by learning to hold a cat without anxiety you'll also alter the content of your thoughts about cats. The same thing is true for other objects of anxiety to which you become "immune" by experience or desensitization. Exposure, when done properly and persistently, helps you to tell yourself the truth in a deep new way—from the heart.

Take cats, for instance. When people have an irrational fear of cats, they may "know" the truth about cats when there isn't a cat within miles. They "know" cats are not dangerous animals. But when they're forced to be in the same room with a feline pet, what they "know" changes.

They will now find they're telling themselves, "That cat is dangerous. It will jump on you, claw you, suck your breath, do you harm." At that moment, it becomes very hard for them to try to tell themselves something else, so strong is their emotional arousal.

After desensitizing themselves, however, they're "convinced" of the truth. Tune in on their self-talk while they hold the kitten and pet it contentedly: "This little thing can't hurt me. Look how he cuddles down in my lap, snuggling as close as he can get. He's actually quite attractive. I can see now that all my fears were overblown! Lord, thank you for making kittens!"

What do phobics tell themselves? Let's take a look at some specific phobic misbeliefs.

Elevator phobia. Usually, the elevator phobic believes there is some safe distance above ground and is willing to ride that distance (for example, to the third floor). But beyond that limit, this kind of self-talk takes over: "The cables will break and the car will crash and hurt me or kill me. This thing will get stuck between floors, the doors won't open, and I'll be trapped. It will be a long wait before help comes! I might starve or suffocate to death."

Albert Ellis has described the misbeliefs of the elevator phobic like this: "I *must* not be inconvenienced or harmed in any way when riding in an elevator. There is at least a slight chance that this kind of horrible inconvenience or harm will occur if I ride in elevators. That would be *terrible.* Therefore I *must not*, under any condition, ride in elevators!" Ellis notes:

A preference is irrationally escalated into an absolutistic demand or command. All people prefer to avoid harm or severe inconvenience when riding in elevators, most of them easily convince themselves that the chances of such accidents occurring are very slight; therefore they are willing to take the risk of using this means of transportation. But as soon as you insist, "I absolutely must not be inconvenienced or harmed in elevators," and there is of course always some chance that you may be, you will bring on feelings of terror or horror about riding in them, and will become phobic about them. Virtually any must leads to feelings of anxiety—unless you are (foolishly) certain that your must will not be fulfilled.[3]

For that reason we may wisely choose to give up our *musts.*

Acrophobia (height phobia). This is a fear of being on high floors of buildings, on tops of hills or mountains, or approaching the edges of bridges or subway tracks. Typical self-talk in this case sounds something like this: "I'll fall off. I'll be badly hurt or killed! In fact, I might get the urge to jump off. I think I can feel something drawing me to the edge now!"

Some acrophobics put their misbeliefs in visual form. They imagine the building tilting and themselves falling off the top. They can even have physical sensations of falling (what Aaron T. Beck has labeled *somatic imaging*).

Claustrophobia (fear of closed places). This is fear verging on terror of being inside tunnels; closets; small, locked rooms; and sometimes crowds. Claustrophobics tell themselves: "I'll suffocate. There won't be enough air. The tunnel will cave in and I'll be buried alive or killed by falling debris."

Sometimes the fear seems so real victims can actually feel shortness of breath when inside the feared space. They believe they can actually sense their chests constricting, feel faint, and experience other frightening bodily sensations (again, this is somatic imaging).

Airplane phobia (fear of flying). This phobia says to the sufferer: "I'll die from deprivation of air in the plane if anything goes wrong. I'll get so anxious up there I'll lose control of myself and cause an accident or be terribly embarrassed." Most often, the self-talk has to do with predicting disaster: "I know the plane will crash and I'll be killed."

The self-talk of people with a phobia changes as their situation changes. Carrie's husband, for example, had begged her to go with him on a business trip to Florida. "We'll spend a few days on the beach in the sun while we're there," he promised, hoping to persuade her.

But Carrie was terrified whenever she thought about getting on an airplane. "When I'm sitting here in your office," she confessed to me, "I know there's less danger flying to Florida than driving home on the freeway. Right now, the chance of a crash seems about one in a million.

"But if I get on a plane, I'll be sure it's going to crash. If we hit rough weather and the plane bounces up and down, I'll tell myself the chances are a hundred to one that we'll die. I'll be sure we've had it!"

Most phobics can tell you without equivocation that the disasters they fear are unlikely, so long as they aren't in the feared situation. But when they are, their beliefs and self-talk do a complete reversal.

These and similar phobic misbeliefs must be replaced with spiritually grounded truth. Otherwise phobic people will go right on telling themselves the feared situation must be avoided at almost any cost. They will plan their lives around that avoidance, leading to a frustrating situation for that living, busy, active faith which ever presses toward fulfillment of God's good plan for their life.

In this case, however, we face a special problem. As we've seen, phobic people tell themselves the truth *when they are not in the feared situation*. It's in the tight spots that they begin to buy into enemy deception and to exercise the scary misbeliefs leading to avoidance.

So how can they bring about the needed change? Perhaps you've guessed: exposure. Either by directly entering their feared situation and staying there until their feelings (and false beliefs) change; or by gentle and gradual *in vivo* desensitization; or by desensitization in imagination: People with phobias may have to change their misbeliefs by experience, by exposing themselves to their feared situations. There, telling themselves the truth vigorously, they will experience it at the same time, and the phobic misbeliefs will change.

What truth must be experienced? Faith will urge two truths in nearly every feared situation. One is a *probability* kind of truth, the other is *spiritual*. In any phobia, the twisted belief that we will almost surely suffer disaster or major inconvenience or unacceptably miserable distress and discomfort must be altered to fit reality. Of course, there is *some* minimal chance that the plane will crash, the kitten will scratch or bite, the elevator will get stuck, or that some nut will come along and push us off the cliff from behind. But it's only *minimal*.

The probability is so low for all these that most people ignore it or dismiss it from their minds. And when phobia victims get better, they too come to the point where, in the formerly feared situation, they can tell themselves in faith, "Yes, I could fall off this balcony, I suppose, but the fact is that the chance of it approaches zero! I refuse to upset myself over probabilities that low."

The *spiritual* kind of truth urged by faith changes phobics' belief that if they should be killed, it would be dreadful, unthinkable, totally inadmissible. The truth for faith is that Christ has abolished death and brought life and immortality to light: that it is sometimes better for us to depart and be with Christ than to stay where we are; and that the sting of death and the victory of the grave have long since been removed and destroyed. Faith engages in this kind of self-talk: "While I'm not planning to die in this airplane, if it were to happen, such an event would only usher me in to a new level of existence where I'll know total and unmixed joy for the very first time ever!"

Similarly, faith's brilliant light appropriately trivializes the inconvenience or discomfort we may have been altering our lives to avoid and puts them in perspective. Faith says: "Of course I could tolerate it if people should think less of me or if the kitten should bite me or if the night's sleep should be less than perfect!"

Our discussion of strategies for overcoming phobia should give you hope if you suffer from phobic responses. If you have irrational anxiety involving certain objects or experiences, you too can work toward changing your self-talk while you're courageously confronting your feared situations—directly, while desensitizing yourself *in vivo*, or during systematic desensitization in imagination.

Panic Attacks and Agoraphobia

It came on without warning—all of a sudden, she felt like she was dying. What was happening to her? What was her body doing? Was she having a heart attack? Was she losing her mind?

The discount store she was in had changed somehow. In a flash, everything had taken on a strange, garish cast. The light was too bright, harsh, as it ricocheted off the walls and the stacks of merchandise. She felt her heart pounding, her skin crawling, her head spinning, becoming too light, as if black cotton were being stuffed into her brain.

Even now she was losing her balance. She held on to a display case to steady herself, sure she was going to fall. Should she cry out for help?

The huge store was full of people. Had any of them noticed? What would they think? She felt like she couldn't talk, wouldn't make sense, would stutter or quaver as she spoke. They'd think she was crazy. She was perspiring as if she'd run a mile or had a fever. She thought she was about to pass out if she didn't get some air—fast.

Was she dying? Maybe she was having a stroke. She had to get outside. She abandoned her half-filled shopping cart and made for the store exit.

Once she was on the street she began walking as fast as she could, sure she would collapse at any moment, but unable to stand still. She wanted to lie down right on the sidewalk. After what seemed forever, she began to feel a little better. The attack subsided. But she knew she couldn't go into that store again.

Maria's first panic attack left her demoralized and defeated. It was the beginning of her bout with *agoraphobia*.

Things might have gone differently. If she had been with her husband, Gil, he would have called an ambulance or taken her to a hospital. Many victims of panic attacks find themselves taken to an emergency room. But some, like Maria, keep their first attack secret, believing it's only more evidence of their incompetence, that others would only think less of them for it.

This story of a sudden first attack of panic has been told and retold with minor variations in every clinician's office. The event signaled the beginning of a most unpleasant time for Maria and Gil, a young couple in their late twenties. Married for only two years, they were still adjusting to each other when their daughter Sonia arrived. Delighted with their new infant, they set about adjusting to her somewhat demanding little presence as well.

Increased Responsibility

Responsibility had always weighed heavily on Maria. She couldn't allow herself to perform less than well at anything without imagining she had failed. Now she suddenly felt responsible not only for her household duties and for Gil's happiness, but for a baby as well. On top of that, she had recently been made manager of the law office where she worked as an assistant. She felt dominated by Gil's strong personality and expectations at home and unequal to the new demands of her job at the office.

Tune in on this young woman's thoughts prior to her first panic attack: "I can't handle everything by myself. I'm not up to raising Sonia; I don't know the first thing about being a mother. I'll probably do something wrong, and harm Sonia for life.

"Gil will see how inept I am and stop loving and respecting me. He'll be unhappy with our marriage and maybe he'll even leave me. Meantime, he's expecting more of me now and he wants me to do everything right. I have to prove myself to him so he'll be pleased with his new wife."

Lately, weary musings on her own inadequacy coupled with

reminders of heavy responsibility had been circulating around and around in Maria's brain. No matter what else she was doing, this monologue on Gil's expectations, her deficiencies, and her overwhelming responsibilities played itself automatically and unremittingly from a tape located somewhere in the shadows of her mind.

Leaning on Another Person

Then came the attack in the discount store. Now Maria had a new preoccupation. The disaster! She'd felt different—terrified—ever since.

Yesterday she got upset at home by herself! The awful feelings had commenced without warning. Was it happening again?

Now she felt raw fear. What if some terrible thing should occur while she was all alone? She couldn't handle it by herself. She called Gil at work.

Gil came home immediately, and his calm reassurance steadied her a bit. He was strong. He would take care of her.

"I'm Weak, Damaged, Helpless!"

But now Maria saw herself as weak, helpless, and vulnerable. The attack could happen anywhere. She could suddenly be squeezed in a crowded store until she couldn't move. She might not be able to breathe. She could be put down or made to feel insignificant. The danger was everywhere!

Now it dawned on her that she was never safe! She could never be all right alone. She needed a strong person with her all the time because something was obviously very wrong. She was so damaged, so incapable of doing anything, so out of control—the victim of nameless internal and external forces.

Too Anxious to . . .

The fear and anxiety caused by all this was enormous. It produced physiological changes Maria would easily detect. To her they meant she was either dying or going crazy. Surely she would faint or have a heart attack or a stroke!

Maria perceived the feelings of anxiety as dangerous in themselves, so she tried to control them, especially when she couldn't avoid going to a store or to some other "dangerous" place. There she would feel intense anxiety so strong she believed she couldn't talk without stammering or her voice shaking. She felt as though she would fall down and have to steady herself against a wall to stay on her feet.

Maria was sure she wouldn't be able to drive without an accident, because she couldn't control the car. Her anxiety, so intense in the store, could turn into a panic attack. So she always needed to escape as soon as possible, to get home where she was "safe" in case of another attack. Soon she avoided going out at all.

All this led to even less of a sense of control. She saw herself as insufficient, and inept. She became sure she was a "loser," completely trapped and controlled by others and by her anxiety.

Agoraphobia Really *Isn't* . . .

What you have just read is a fairly typical "homogenized"[1] account of the onset of one person's *agoraphobia with panic attacks* (the official title of this disorder in the diagnostic manual). *Agoraphobia* wasn't listed in the last chapter as a phobia because it really isn't one. If you're a victim of agoraphobia, you might wish it were. Then you could, like other phobics, encapsulate your fear feelings, attach them to some avoidable object, and go on with life. But you can't do that.

Neither is the disorder "fear of the marketplace"—which is what the Greek root *agora* implies—an actual phobia. The problem was once thought to be phobia of the open spaces and stores in the "marketplace." But we now are painfully aware that what is actually feared is being alone or being in a public place, such as a crowded restaurant or store from which escape would be difficult or where help would not be available in case of a sudden attack. This problem usually begins after a panic attack.

The First Panic Attack, and Agoraphobia

The first attack of panic often occurs in those whose already shaky sense of competence has been strained by increased responsibility or perhaps the loss of someone strong and important in their lives. Many experts believe that from the first attack on, such patients live in terror of another attack. They especially fear the outcome, which they tell themselves would be death or incapacitation.

If you've had a panic attack, you can appreciate why victims are shaken to the core by it. You know how it feels, with symptoms like these:

> rapid heart beat
> trembling
> abdominal pain
> lightheadedness
> sweating
> feeling of imminent collapse
> depersonalization (feeling of not being "there")
> derealization (feeling things aren't real)
> chest pains
> feeling of inability to control own mind
> hyperventilation
> inner trembling
> weakness
> dizziness
> feeling of imminent loss of balance or consciousness

Anyone who has not experienced any of this can, with a little imagination, grasp the terror felt by those who have. No wonder that from this episode on the first goal in life becomes prevention of another panic attack! Agoraphobics aim to stay away from any place where an attack might happen or where they might feel unable to get help in case one did happen. For all the agoraphobics I've seen personally (and that's quite a large number—maybe fifty or so), the real fear is not of the marketplace, but of the next panic episode and of having it without access to help.

Interpreting the Symptoms

Not only are the symptoms of agoraphobia frightening, people almost invariably interpret them as menacing in the extreme. Remember, the self-talk with which we interpret what's happening to us can be our major problem. And remember, too, it's spontaneous and unintentional.

We don't deliberately decide to tell ourselves terrible stories and alarming untruths. They just pop into our head by themselves. So it's important to recognize them for what they are and to know that we and our faith can stop them.

If you've experienced panics, which of the following misbeliefs do you tell yourself in interpreting them?

Misbeliefs about the symptoms:

"I'm having a mental breakdown."
"I'm having a physical collapse."
"I'm choking to death."
"I'm having a heart attack."
"I'm having a stroke."
"I'll lose control and hurt someone/hurt myself/scream/be unable to keep the car on the road/go insane/kill someone/disgrace myself."

Images of Terror

Experiments have determined that for many people with agoraphobia, misbeliefs take the form of *imagery*, not just *words*. This imagery pops into mind as involuntarily as verbal misbeliefs. Those who are "imagers" create mental pictures of themselves fainting, being humiliated, getting into a terrible accident when out of control, falling to the ground, even dying.[2] Whether they are words or pictures in their head, all these are *beliefs* and all of them are *erroneous* beliefs. None of these things ever happen.[3]

Self-Talk in Fear-Filled Settings

Tune in on your self-talk when you think you're in one of your own danger spots. You probably bring on your own panic with spontaneous alarm thoughts like these:

"I am now in a place where something terrible can happen to me."

"These terrible episodes can happen suddenly and with no sign that they're coming. So it's dangerous for me to be alone here because I doubt I could easily get help if I needed it."

"I must have a sturdy, strong person with me because he or she could help me if something happened."

"What's that? A change in my heartbeat? A pain in my chest? A tightening in my stomach? It could mean another one is starting. What if it gets worse and I die before I can get it stopped?"

You can see how allowing such notions to reign in your mind without contradiction will tighten you up. And as you continue letting them pound themselves in, they'll tighten you up even more, until you're so tense and anxious it's as if you virtually throw the switches of your autonomic nervous system on full power.

But all this self-talk simply has the effect of increasing the symptoms. This insight is important for your recovery. You only descend deeper into panic with such erroneous notions, repeated again and again in your internal speech. Telling yourself that you must never have another panic attack, that you have to do whatever is necessary to keep panic from overtaking you, that you therefore cannot allow yourself to feel the slightest bit of anxiety—all this only makes you more tense and more panicky!

Agoraphobic Avoidance

What agoraphobics fear and try to avoid is *any* situation where they are *alone* and *likely to have difficulty getting help.* That's why they often avoid stores, restaurants, driving, church services, crowds, even hair salons, dentists' and doctors' offices, theaters, trains, planes, buses. Sometimes they also fear going anywhere at all *alone.*

Notice the pivotal role of *avoidance* in this disorder. Like other people who are troubled by anxiety, like all of us, I suppose, to some extent, agoraphobics try to handle anxiety by avoidance and wind up creating more problems for themselves. Why? By making themselves believe they are weak, helpless, and about to collapse from panic when there is no objective danger, they undermine their belief in their own sense of sufficiency, or adequacy to endure, survive, and cope.

In this way agoraphobics become, in their own eyes, less and less capable of even making it through the simplest situations. This of course is not a matter of lowliness or humility, which result from a truthful self-image. Instead, this is a totally false and destructive assessment by victims of their own ability to function.

What You Can Do About It

Often the agoraphobic feels deserted by God, insecure, and alone. "If God really were with me," they reason, "surely I wouldn't feel all this fear and panic!" They try to read the Bible and sometimes find even the words of Scripture threatening, reminding them of their sinfulness or inadequacy. So they begin avoiding Scripture too. They think their prayers aren't answered, so they may avoid prayer as well. Talking to God becomes for them only a reminder of their wretchedness.

Even so, however deeply it may be buried under layers of misbelief and terrifying mental images, they may have faith in Jesus Christ as their Savior, Lord, and healer. They may know, in that faith, that He will heal them and that they will be free from their misery.

If this is your situation, remember: No matter how many false ideas to the contrary may be rattling around in your head, no matter how loudly your misbeliefs may try to shout down the voice of faith, deep inside you somewhere your buried faith is living. That faith desires to be busy and active, doing the will of your dear Father without fear and hesitation. Liberate the voice of this faith and attend to its impulses—you'll need it to get through the difficult steps involved in getting better.

Six Steps Toward Living Again

What can you do to overcome this type of anxiety? I recommend six steps:

1. Liberate your faith and listen to it as it urges you to focus on responding to God. Recognize that what you've been avoiding may be what God wills for you to do. This means you must stop demanding to be anxiety-free before you ever start.

You may hope that all you have to do is chat with a therapist for a few weeks, months, or even years, and then, at the end of your last session, walk out so calm and collected that no pain will ever occur again. But that's not likely to happen. You must in faith set your heart on accepting whatever anxiety is necessary for as long as it is necessary. You must set your sights on *doing God's will* rather than *feeling totally calm and anxiety free.* This seems a paradox, I agree, but it's the fastest route to being free.

2. Practice deep relaxation every day, or even twice each day (or more if you are so tense you need several sessions to remain reasonably unwound; see chapter 9). Not only will regular relaxation practice break the hold of anxiety during the time you're practicing it, but it will also progressively lower your general tension level—a sorely needed step.

3. Take other measures which have been found to reduce physical tension. Stop using pulse-quickening caffeine (found not only in coffee but also in soft drinks and headache remedies; check labels).[4] See that your diet is light on junk foods and heavy on vegetables, whole grains, fruits, and protein-rich foods.

Finally, take part in vigorous aerobic exercise like running, bicycling, cross-country skiing, and stair climbing. You can get the particulars from numerous sources, including the American Heart Association.[5] Several studies have demonstrated that regular aerobic exercise reduces stress, tension, and anxiety. If you're over forty or have heart disease, discuss any contemplated exercise program with your physician before starting.

4. Listen to your faith even if the sound of its voice seems very faint as it leads you into *doing* the very things you have been *avoiding*, the things that the anxious part of you *doesn't want to do*. Construct a hierarchy of scenes you now avoid, beginning with easy items and working up to the more difficult. Then, instead of desensitizing yourself in imagination, do it *in vivo* (in reality).

Construct your hierarchy so that, at first, your strong helpful person goes with you into the situations. Then, as you go along, carry out your scenes alone. Gradually move up to the more difficult scenes, doing them alone until there are no more situations you're avoiding. Even if you still feel some anxiety, you must continue to do them if you want to be well.

5. But what about that fear and anxiety? Agoraphobics have to work especially hard at replacing their threatening self-talk with the truth because it's their misbeliefs about what will happen to them that prevent their carrying out the fourth step very effectively. In other words, you have to believe you will *not* encounter a terrible catastrophe as a result of your panic and anxiety.

Let's make this reality plain: Don't tell yourself, "I won't have any more panic or anxiety." You may! In fact, any of us may. Anxiety and even panic under some conditions are part of life.

Instead, you must say: "If I get anxious or even panicky, I'll do what I can to calm down. But it isn't essential for me to never have any of those feelings. I'll carry on anyway."

You'll have to tell yourself the truth about all those threats of what will happen to you. Here's the critical fact: "It's not true that panic will lead to some dreadful catastrophic event. I won't die or go crazy or collapse. At worst, I'll feel uncomfortable."

6. Some people with panic attacks can be helped enormously with appropriate medication. The really good news about this is that, for some reason, the best and most effective medication for panic attacks is *not* tranquilizers (which are habit forming, addictive, and usually of doubtful value for this condition), but *antidepressants* (which are not addictive and rarely even habit-forming). Your physician or psychiatrist will be able to help you decide whether medication is likely to be helpful to you.

If you have trouble with panic and agoraphobia, listen to your faith. As you let faith drive and motivate your thinking and behavior, let faith's emphasis on responsibility become sweet to you as it encourages you to gird yourself for spiritual battles. Though it may seem impossible now, I know that you can take these first steps, until you are marching boldly into the face of every fear that would cripple you.

How to (Almost) Stop Worrying

Some people experience most of their anxiety in their minds rather than as strong physiological anxiety. In other words, they worry. We've referred to this in an earlier chapter as *mental anxiety*. Let me tell you about a "worry" experience of my own.

The first sign of trouble appeared on a bright, sunny Tuesday morning. I was listening to a client describe the farm on which he'd grown up when I glanced at my license to practice psychology in Minnesota hanging on the wall over my desk—one of those trappings of daily life you have always before your eyes but never see. For some reason I noticed the renewal date.

Something seemed wrong, very wrong, I forced myself to attend to the client, but no sooner was the session over than I raced back to check what I thought I had noticed. Sure enough, something *was* wrong. My license was no longer current. It had expired six months before!

I was certain I had sent the renewal fee—or had I? Was it possible I hadn't? How could I have neglected such a critical detail?

I looked through every drawer and file where I thought there might be a record of my having paid the renewal fee. Nowhere was it to be found! I was practicing psychology without a license. I was breaking the law—unless—unless Candy had sent the renewal fee and we had a canceled check to prove it.

She was sure she'd sent the check six months ago—or had she? Maybe she had and the renewal confirmation never arrived. That night we reviewed our check stubs. No. There had been *no renewal*! It was true. I was practicing with no right to do so. I could be in big trouble!

Did I worry? You bet! Anxiety seeped out of my pores! I tormented myself, rehearsing the awful possibilities.

What if they revoked my license? Barred me from practice forever? What if I were forced to reimburse all the fees I'd collected during those unlicensed six months?

I'd be ruined. How would our family live? Pay the mortgage? Help the kids through school? What about the disgrace? I could see nothing but dreadful consequences ahead.

Suddenly, in the midst of all this worrying, I asked myself, "What am I doing? I'm just making myself wretched with worry, feeding myself this rubbish without knowing for sure that any of it is so! I know some facts, things that *are* so! And the most important facts are these: God is in charge of this. *His arm is not shortened.* The Lord is my Shepherd. . . . What can man do to me?

"Even if God has chosen to discipline me through some hardship, it will be up to me to get the good out of it, not to collapse with worry. Moreover, my first objective must be to maintain a serene, peaceful spirit. That's even more important than whether or not I renew my license."

Whew! I felt better immediately. The heat was off. The sense of relief was marked. The truth worked the way it's supposed to. I slept well.

How to Make Worries Snowball

I wish every one of my worrying clients would give themselves energetically to the truth! In my experience, worried Christians nearly always hear biblical teaching about worry in the wrong way. They take God's worry-healing medicine as if it were toxic!

I've met stewing Christians who construe God's promises and guarantees as a law with which to threaten and castigate themselves. Jesus' words "Do not worry" (Matthew 6:25–34), for instance, come across to some people only as a stern demand backed up with implied threats—a legal injunction with painful consequences for disobedience. They imagine Jesus saying, "You're worrying again! I can't accept you as long as you keep right on disobeying me. Haven't I ordered you to stop that wicked worrying?"

They think they can't stop, so they pile condemnation on themselves when they hear these passages. The way they see it, any time they're anxious, they're being disobedient and bringing more woe on themselves! So they cause their worrying to snowball.

But are these and other Bible teachings about worry really only a set of tough regulations? Aren't they rather to be taken as gospel—as good news? Here, instead of threatening commands we can't possibly carry out by merely wanting to, is teaching, help, therapy, material we can incorporate into fresh, powerful self-talk by which God and His truth can free us from anxiety and worry.

Who's in Charge Here, Anyway?

You don't have to be ultimately responsible for yourself. You can do what you can do and then leave the outcome to God, who will take responsibility for you as a caring and omnipotent Father. Self-talk must be saturated with the truth that once you've let your request be made known to God, *nothing is ever again the same.* To those who understand God as He means to be understood, that's only good news.

Take my brother-in-law, Eugene Faszholz, for example. Not long ago he was lying on his back in the hospital recovering from angioplasty—a surgical procedure in which a tiny balloon is fed up through a large artery into a plaque-narrowed blood vessel and inflated to allow more blood to flow to the heart. He'd been warned that the vessel might close up again within twenty-four hours, with disastrous results.

Worry and anxiety tormented him. He told himself, "I'm an athlete. I've always made my body do whatever I've wanted it to and my body responded. But now when I tell myself I *must* stop being anxious and

stressing myself, I can't force myself to do it." The more he told himself
he ought to control his anxiety, the worse it got.

Then God spoke to him: "Who's in charge here, Gene?"

"You are, God," Gene answered meekly.

With that the truth dawned on him. At the same moment, a mighty
wave of peace washed over his mind, and his tormented thoughts came
to rest. Why? Because this word was the good news so often overlooked
by worriers: the news that he didn't have to heal and save himself from
his situation—that his well-being was entirely in the hands of a loving,
merciful and all-capable Person.

It's good news that there's nothing we can do. It's a big relief that
we can let God do it. It's a gift, like getting walked to first base instead
of having to get a hit.

For that reason, "Have no anxiety about anything," "Don't think
about tomorrow," and the other scriptural teachings about anxiety are
gospel: They announce freedom to us. We don't *have* to get anxious!
They are not *law* berating us for being such a poor excuse for a Christian if we happen to be worried!

Mental Lists of "What ifs . . ."

When Christians feel unable to stop worrying, it's because they
haven't begun doing what's powerfully effective against worry. Worriers
habitually and routinely place the worst possible construction on every
situation. Yet situations, circumstances, and events in themselves have
no power to upset us.

"Men are disturbed," said the stoic philosopher Epictetus, "not
by things, but by the view they take of them." Worriers take the most
catastrophic view conceivable when they interpret to themselves the
meaning of events. They explain their misfortunes by telling themselves
they can never win, they always make things go wrong, and they lack
competence. So they're worthless. They predict unfailingly that events
will come to the most negative conceivable conclusion.

In keeping with this habit of choosing the most negative possible explanation, worriers find themselves making mental lists of all the adverse things that might occur. They mentally catalogue everything they can think of that could possibly go wrong. For worriers, the sentences in their inner speech all begin with "What if . . . ?" followed by a negative possibility.

Do What You Can

If you're a worrier, you can find help! Here's what you must do: Take the reins away from the devil and the flesh, and put them firmly into the hands of your *faith*. Faith, you will recall, is living, busy, and active, not passive, not sitting around fussing. So proceed in faith.

First, consider any steps you're able to take for cure and prevention. Then take them. This may seem self-evident, but many worriers keep themselves stuck in their worry tar pits, not even thinking about taking the remedial or preventive actions available to them.

Ben tormented himself with the thought, "What if I have a heart attack?" I asked him if his physician had found his heart to be especially weak. "I don't know. I haven't seen her in a few years," he said.

"Go and get a good physical exam and ask particularly about your heart," I suggested. "If it's in bad shape, you want to know it so you can take appropriate care of yourself."

Ben hesitated. He'd long avoided discovering what he'd told himself would surely be the awful, terrible truth. (He had put the worst possible interpretation on events.)

But Ben saw his physician anyway. She told him he was in great shape, with the reasons for her conclusion. Result: Ben stopped fussing about having a heart attack and his worrying and nervousness diminished greatly.

We should note that Ben wasn't quite as severe a worrier as some. Other worriers might have listened to the doctor and then told

THE GOOD NEWS ABOUT WORRY

themselves, "She's just saying all that to make me feel better. She knows my case is hopeless and I'm probably doomed."

If you too are a worrier about your physical condition, suspend fussing about your health until you get good information from your physician. Then do what you can to stay well or to get better.

Are you fretting about failing a driver's test but still wanting a license? Don't keep putting off the moment of truth: Go and take the test.

Are you wishing you could pass a course in trigonometry or Russian, but telling yourself you might fail—so you put off a decision to get started? Go in faith and do it!

Do you torture yourself about the awful disasters likely to occur if you were to serve dinner to your boss and his wife, wishing all the time you could bring it off with a flourish? Do you keep making excuses for not giving a testimony in church because you worry about speaking in public? Instead of putting off the ordeal, let your living, busy, active faith move you into taking it in hand and doing it.

Are you worrying about money? What have you done to budget your expenses or increase your income? Are you worrying that others might not like you? Learn what you can from books on how to win friends or from communications training courses.

You get the point: Take action!

First, Pray—and Here's Why

First among the potent, effective actions faith will lead us to take is *prayer.* Is prayer likely to help? Absolutely. Prayer that is faith-directed has a phenomenal track record as an effective step to take when we're worried. Here are four incontrovertible reasons for turning to prayer in faith and for expecting that it will change things about which we're worried:

- God *commands* us to pray: "Call upon me in the day of trouble," He says. "I will deliver you, and you will honor me" (Psalm 50:15).

God has made us and bought us, so believing Christians have committed their lives to obeying Him. Even if prayer produced no results, the fact that God himself directs us to do it would be enough to make it the first action to take when we worry. He is God. Obey Him.

- God *promises* to hear and answer prayer. The passage we just looked at from Psalm 50 exemplifies His standing promise. Jesus' own teaching includes His pledge that prayer will produce results, and that if we ask, we'll receive (Matthew 7:7-8). The Bible contains so many assurances from God that He answers prayer that a person reading them carefully soon realizes the Holy Spirit means business in this matter.[1]

- Many *case histories* recorded in the Bible and in biographical anecdotes from various sources furnish stunning examples of God's hearing and answering prayer. The poor Canaanite woman prayed noisily for her daughter with the result that the girl was delivered (see Matthew 15:22-28). The leper prayed for mercy and was cleansed (see Luke 5:12-13). Elijah experienced a dramatic outcome when he prayed for heavenly fire to fall on the Lord's altar (see 1 Kings 18:17-40).

  The fascinating story of Rees Howells, a Welsh coal miner whose ministry of intercession brought spectacular results, has been told by Norman Grubb.[2] Particularly riveting are Grubb's accounts of the effects on specific battles during World War II caused by the powerful prayers of Howells and others in his fellowship. Smith Wigglesworth, George Mueller, G. C. Bevington, Kathryn Kuhlman, Basilea Schlink, Father Francis MacNutt, Brother Andrew, Don Basham, Watchman Nee, and many, many others have written remarkable accounts of answered prayer.[3]

- *Scientific research* has demonstrated prayer's effectiveness. The most striking experiment with prayer I have seen is a carefully designed and executed, controlled research trial by Dr. Randolph C. Byrd of the Cardiology Division, San Francisco General

Medical Center, and the Department of Medicine, University of California, San Francisco. This study was unusually convincing because its design was what scientists refer to as "double blind." When researchers speak of a "double blind" experiment, they mean that neither the subjects nor the people who had any contact with the subjects know which ones were getting the treatment being studied and which were not. So any effects of suggestion on the outcome are ruled out.

In this case the treatment was daily prayer by committed Christian volunteers for the patients in the treatment group. There was also a control group of patients for whom no prayer was offered by volunteers during the experiment. The groups were randomly chosen and volunteers prayed at home, having no contact whatever with any of the patients. The results: Patients who were prayed for did better on all counts. They required less assistance with breathing and fewer medications, and they were in better condition throughout the experiment than the control group.[4]

Prayer works. So do something that's likely to help. The first step faith calls you to is to pray.

What Faith Does Next: Find the Truth

Any situation includes many factors over which we have absolutely no control. So after you take what action you can, then ask yourself, "What's the most positive possible construction I can put on this situation?"

Go over in your mind possible interpretations that are positive and still square with the facts. You don't have to distort reality, change facts, or take leave of logic. Interpretations of the same set of facts can usually vary enormously.

For example, say you expected your spouse to be home a half hour ago, but he hasn't come home and hasn't called. If you're a worrier you'll tell yourself, "He's had a terrible accident; he's probably injured or dead. I'll be all alone. How can I manage?"

But you could just as well adopt a positive (and more likely) explanation for yourself: "He's under the protection of my heavenly Father. He's probably just held up at the office and hasn't had a chance to call. He'll very likely be home any minute now." Which interpretation of the facts do you think would give you more peace?

Most often, the positive interpretation is the one more likely to be true! Stress symptoms are *not* indicative of heart trouble. Late spouses usually *don't* owe their delays to terrible accidents. A letter from the IRS normally *doesn't* mean they are coming to seize your automobile. And Christian faith assures you the bottom line is that God is in charge for good—for your good!

Tell yourself the truth about events and factors you can't do anything about. There is always some point at which you can no longer control things. For example, another person's choices must be beyond your direct control. Similarly, the weather, the course of a disease, the decisions of tyrants around the world, and much else, though often important to you, cannot be influenced by you. In fact, if you tried to list all the factors impinging on your life over which you have little or no control, the list would be endless. Meanwhile, your fretting will not increase your control one bit.

That you aren't in charge might seem disheartening. But assuming you're a Christian, your faith knows and trusts the One who really is in charge, the God who is absolutely reliable and faithful and who loves you beyond anything you can imagine.

Question, Debate, Argue

Many worriers believe they can't break their habit of choosing the negative. But research shows you can! What can you do instead of worrying? First, you can *dispute your negative interpretations*.

By this we mean you can remember and tell yourself who is in charge, replacing your worry thoughts with the truth. Instead of fretting over what you can't control, write out your worry statements. Then ask yourself challenging questions about them. Finally, argue against them and for positive truthful explanations. Debate them energetically! Following are some examples of how to do it.

Stop Worrying About Worry

Some people worry about their anxiety itself! They tell themselves: "If I don't get over my anxiety this time, after reading this book or seeing this doctor or receiving this prayer ministry, then it's hopeless. I'll never get better. I'll probably feel awful for the rest of my life.

"I'll feel even worse than before because I won't have any hope left. Then my wife will get tired of me being this way and she'll leave me. My kids won't respect me. I'll be the cause of it all. I've just *got* to get better this time."

When that happens, here's what to do: First, *ask challenging questions.* Who says this is your last chance? What evidence do you have that your wife and kids don't respect you? How do you know your wife will leave you if you don't stop worrying? Isn't it true that, though you'd *like* to get better as a result of this, nobody in authority has told you you've *got* to get better right now or else?

Second, *argue for the truth with emphasis and vigor.* Don't simply rattle off negations to your misbeliefs such as "This isn't my last chance. It won't be hopeless. I will get better. My wife won't get tired of me."

Instead, come up with positive, truthful interpretations like these: "If this doesn't work, at least I won't be back where I started. I will have ruled out this approach, so that I can begin looking for another. No one ever stays the same for the rest of his life. My wife hasn't said a word about getting tired of me or leaving me if I don't make it this time! The *truth* is, if I don't get better this time, I'll be disappointed, but not wiped out!"

Stop Worrying About Other People

Some folks are inveterate *social worriers.* They never stop threatening themselves with the specter of other people's unfavorable reactions to them. They tell themselves misbeliefs like these:

- "If I talk about my faith, the people at the office won't like me, and will think I'm too religious."
- "I shouldn't have told Simon I couldn't go bike riding with him. He might think I don't like outdoor activities and decide not to ask me out again."
- "I'm afraid to tell Josie how angry I get when she brings her boyfriend to our apartment to sleep with her. She might think I'm a prude."
- "What if the salesman thinks I'm too cheap to buy the highest-priced model?"
- "What if my boss finds out I get anxious? Will I get fired?"

In situations like these, here's what to do. First, as suggested before, *ask challenging questions.* Do *you* dislike people because they're genuinely committed to living a life of faith and love? If not, why do you assume *others* will? What makes you think Simon jumps to conclusions like that? Do you have any evidence that he does? What if Josie *does* think your morals aren't as loose as hers? Whatever she thinks about that, don't you have a responsibility to confront this issue?

What practical difference will it make in your life if the salesperson thinks you're cheap? What do you care what he thinks? How many people have you ever heard of who got fired for being anxious?

Once again, the second step is to *argue for the positive truth with emphasis and vigor.* If you talk about your faith naturally and in a loving, winning manner, most people will accept you. If they don't, they don't. You can't please everybody. So be yourself as you are in Christ and take what comes!

If Simon doesn't call you again, there's no law against your calling him! You could even propose a bike ride!

Even if Josie decides your morals are too stringent for her, the worse she can do is move out; and there are always other people looking for roommates. Maybe this time you can find a Christian roommate. Check the bulletin board at church.

Surely you don't imagine that salesperson goes home and dwells on what a cheapskate you are because you bought his low-priced model! He's just glad you bought *something*!

Most bosses would try to help if they knew you became anxious and uncomfortable. Your boss would probably surprise you if you told him about these feelings! He doesn't want to fire you because he doesn't want to see himself as an unsympathetic ogre, and besides, he knows how productive you are!

Stop Worrying About "Ought-to's"

Some worriers excel in laying false obligations or guilt on themselves. Their worry self-talk abounds with "I should" or "I shouldn't." Typically, they're not worrying about obeying a commandment of God. Instead they put themselves under some human-made law rather than rejoicing in the freedom conferred on them by the gospel (as in Romans 13:8, "Owe no one anything except to love one another" NKJV). Consider these examples of false obligation or guilt:

- "I should return the favor."
- "I should do better than I do."
- "I should always do my best."
- "I should always achieve."
- "I should accomplish more."
- "I shouldn't make mistakes."
- "I should never be late."
- "I have to be better than everybody else at everything."
- "I ought to feel good all of the time."

In these situations you can once again take the same two steps. First, *ask challenging questions.* Where did God say all favors must be returned with precise equality? *Why* do I have to do better than I do at *this*? What makes it imperative for me to achieve? What if I don't achieve all the time? What will happen? Who says I have to accomplish more than I do?

Why is it wrong for me to make a mistake? Do any Scripture passages teach that nobody must ever make a mistake? Why aren't there times when being late is perfectly all right or even preferable? Aren't there times when it doesn't make any difference if I'm *not* better than others? Did Jesus ever insist I must always feel good?

Second, *argue energetically for the truth*. Don't just automatically turn your misbeliefs into negations. Think the issue out. Give yourself positive and stimulating reasons for your truths.

Some favors can't be returned because the people who did them aren't accessible. Sometimes people do favors because they already feel indebted to you, so they don't expect a return. It might be nice to do better than I do in some things, but it won't land me in jail if I don't. There are times when the results of achieving or being best or doing my best just aren't worth the effort, so it's not true that "I must always . . ."

I can make mistakes and most mistakes aren't very important. I can, if I want to, deliberately be late for some things with *no* negative consequences. My feelings are the results of my self-talk and my physiological condition, so I can expect that at times they won't be pleasant. When I have to endure unpleasant feelings, I may be learning how not to be quite so upset by events next time.

Chop Off Your Worry Thoughts

In addition to arguing against your misbeliefs and for the truth, you can do more about stopping worry. Another tactic is to *interrupt your worry thoughts*. Imitating the examples above, you can talk back to your worry thoughts, exercising your faith, engaging your mind and heart with the truth.

Feel free to interrupt your worry thoughts. If you can make them stillborn, so much the better. Chop them off with challenging questions like those above.

Reconstruct the worry thoughts until they argue for the truth before they even get a chance to occupy space in your heart. Then turn your mind onto something else that grabs your interest. Do this as often as necessary to stop the worry habit.

Do What You Fear

Finally, expose yourself to the truly innocuous things you worry about. Remember that faith moves us to forge ahead, to encounter what we must to respond to God. Try deliberately experiencing what you worry about. Remember how avoidance preserves anxiety and even makes it worse. See if you can find a way to expose yourself either all at once or gradually to the things you tell yourself are so threatening.

Exposing yourself might mean deliberately resolving to do what you worry about doing. For example, make a point of not returning a favor for a while. Actually work at not doing "your best" at some tasks.

Skim the newspaper instead of reading every line carefully. Serve a dinner for guests with a deliberately simple menu: instead of shrimp or prime rib, try serving a basic stew or pasta dish. Try not to achieve anything for a whole day, half a day, an hour, ten minutes. Go into some stores and ask for change for a twenty-dollar bill without buying anything.

If you worry about elevators getting stuck, set aside a half day each week to do nothing but ride elevators all over town and keep it up until you aren't worried anymore. If you worry about people rejecting you for being anxious, pick someone to tell about your feelings and let them in on the secret. You might want to reveal your anxiety to numerous friends or coworkers, one by one, noticing how much less worried you are with each revelation.

A caution: Don't get so rewarded by telling others your worries that your needle sticks and you talk about nothing else. You don't want to turn yourself into a professional counselee.

If you can't find a creative way to expose yourself to the thing you worry about in actuality, try letting your imagination do it. After you learn to relax as instructed in chapter 9, construct scenes in which you imagine yourself doing what you fear. Then get yourself deeply relaxed and visualize the scenes one at a time until you aren't worried about them anymore.

You may find after all this that you need some help from a professional psychotherapist. If so, there's nothing wrong with getting it! Worry and anxiety, if they seem beyond what you can cope with by yourself, will very likely give way to effective therapy.

If you're a Christian, you can obtain the names of some Christian psychologists or therapists, give them a phone call, and ask what kinds of treatment they do for worry. If what they suggest resembles the material in this book, make an appointment with the one you think you'll work best with, and have a session to see if you think you can make progress with that person. You'll be glad you did: Currently treatment methods are generally quite effective for worry and anxiety.

Contentment, Happiness, and Faith

Worrying prevents happiness because it prevents living in the present. I've noticed how much of what the news media concentrate their attention on is not news about what has happened recently, but what experts think *will* happen. And the predictions are usually negative—just like the predictions of the worrier! Furthermore, these experts' predictions, like those of worriers, are most often wrong.

The French philosopher Blaise Pascal also observed that the worrier attends to the future, to what *will* happen (or, occasionally, to the past—to what he or she did wrong). Just as attending to the latest news almost never improves our mood, so being a worrier usually prevents our enjoying happiness. Happiness comes from contentment with the present.

Research has shown that, so far as happiness is concerned, it doesn't matter whether you're rich or poor, sighted or blind, quadriplegic or unimpaired, sick or well, hairy or bald, short or tall. What does matter is whether you're contented and living in the present.[5] Faith, in contrast to worrying, is living in the *now*, leaving the mistakes of the past under the Cross, and the concerns of the future to Him who even now is in charge of it.

Usually, we discover that all our worrying was for nothing. For example, remember the flap about the license renewal I had overlooked? I called the license board office and discovered I was right to conclude that I had not renewed. But the board secretary didn't act as though that was so unusual. She said she'd send me a bill for the renewal fee plus a reasonable charge for late renewal.

"That's it?" I asked, incredulous.

"Yes, Dr. Backus, that's it."

What a waste of energy my worrying had been!

Faith Can Overcome

Twenty-six-year-old Kyle had never had a date because he was afraid to ask anyone to go out with him. After we worked for a while on Kyle's pesky assumption that there was no way a desirable girl would want to consider him as a boyfriend, he steadied his trembling hand one evening and punched the phone number of the elegant brunette he'd recently met at a concert. Fifteen minutes later he had a date.

Eight and a half months after that, Kyle and Kim were married. Kyle has also challenged and overcome a couple of other similar avoidance habits. Along with attacking his misbeliefs, this approach caused the old fear that others, particularly attractive and desirable others, would surely rebuff him, to diminish considerably.

Perhaps you've wondered what happened to some of the people you read about in earlier chapters. Could they, by faith, also manage to defy their strong avoidance habits and challenge the misbeliefs supporting them? They could, and some did.

212

Remember Cal, in chapter 2? He thought long and hard about surrendering the deceptive feelings of security he gained from avoiding his friends from church. Cal saw clearly that the only road to freedom lay through trepidation, so he chose to take a step-by-step approach to rejoining the human race. It wasn't easy for him to return for increasingly longer periods to church gatherings, but as he did so, challenging his misbeliefs energetically, his faith gradually overcame old avoidance habits and his anxiety in church gatherings continued to diminish.

Ava, whom you also met in chapter 2, once firmly believed she couldn't stand the anxiety and panic she might experience without being attended wherever she went by her husband, Paul. She had manipulated Paul into a kind of tandem neurosis with her so that he too believed she simply had to be accompanied wherever she went. It was thus important for both of them to work together to challenge their misbeliefs about Ava's need for constant "help."

They did, and Ava worked out a series of ventures she would attempt without Paul while Paul forced himself to stop expressing his very unhelpful misgivings. At first, Ava tried easy ventures such as trips to the convenience store a block from home. As her ventures progressed in difficulty, she managed to prove to herself and Paul that she could do whatever she wished without demanding his presence. By faith she dared to do what she feared most—to go places alone. As far as I know, she and Paul are both still free of their old problem.

Some may believe all these victories pale beside the dauntless courage of the martyrs listed in Hebrews 11, who by faith did epic deeds of bravery. And by objective standards it's true that the martyrs faced real danger while those defying anxiety often brave only their own painful feelings. But I'm thrilled and impressed nevertheless every time I see ordinary people disregard distressing fears and venture into what are to them terrifying situations so they can overcome misbeliefs and avoidance habits. In one important respect they're like the martyrs: They are exercising a genuine faith in the God whose promises are more real to them than their own pounding hearts. And they are trusting Him with a faith that is genuinely living, busy, and active!

Can you imagine having the same victory in your own life? Perhaps not without help. But you *can* have help. Jesus has promised that our Father will send the Holy Spirit to those who ask, and that the Spirit will come as the "counselor" or "comforter" (see John 14). This biblical word for the Spirit literally means "the one who comes and stays alongside" you. What many others have found, what you can discover for yourself, is that you can have Him alongside you to keep you in the truth as you challenge the misbeliefs and avoidances in your own life.

A Prayer for Help

"Father, I'm tired of giving in to anxiety, sick of living my life by avoidance, ready to let my faith become living, busy, and active to overcome. But, Lord, I don't see how I can do it without your Holy Spirit. Send Him, Father, to take that place alongside me when I step out to conquer my own avoidance. I don't expect you simply to dissolve my anxiety with no effort on my part. But I do expect you to supply the courage to face and endure even if the way to freedom is hard. In Jesus' name. Amen."

NOTES

CHAPTER 1

1. Hans Selye, M.D., *Stress Without Distress* (New York: Signet, 1974).

CHAPTER 2

1. Jeffrey Scott Steffenson, *Communication Anxiety*, unpublished dissertation, Master of Arts, University of Minnesota, Duluth, 1990, p. 4.

2. *Anxiety: The Endless Crisis* (Audiotape), published by Center for Cassette Studies, 38588.

3. Ernest Becker, *The Denial of Death* (New York: The Free Press, 1973.)

CHAPTER 3

1. We discussed *misbeliefs* and their role in producing anxiety in chapter one.

2. See, for example, John Theodore Mueller, *Christian Dogmatics* (St. Louis: Concordia Publishing House, 1934), p. 322.

3. Dietrich Bonhoeffer, tr. R. H. Fuller, *The Cost of Discipleship* (New York: Macmillan, 1957), pp. 50, 69.

4. This widely quoted selection is a part of Luther's great *Preface to the Epistle to the Romans* (1522). It is quoted here from *The Works of Martin Luther*, the Philadelphia Edition, Volume VI (Philadelphia: Muhlenberg Press, 1932), pp. 451–52.

5. To read about some of the groundbreaking experiments on this problem, see R. L. Solomon and L. C. Wynne, "Traumatic Avoidance Learning: The Principles of Anxiety Conservation and Partial Irreversibility," *Psychology Review*, 61, 1954, pp. 353–85.

CHAPTER 5

1. See, for example, Proverbs 22:6: "Train a child in the way he should go, and when he is old he will not turn from it." Compare also Ephesians 6:4. Behavior psychologists (largely ignored by Christian counselors) have provided a good deal of information about how to do such training effectively.
2. Romans 6:20–23. Note especially, "But now that you have been set free from sin and have become slaves to God, the benefit you reap leads to holiness, and the result is eternal life."
3. Read Romans 6–8 for a thorough discussion of these two natures and the conflict between them experienced by every believer. Two additional resources for those who would like to pursue this subject further: Anders Nygren, tr. Carl C. Rasmussen, *Commentary on Romans* (Philadelphia: Muhlenberg Press, 1949), pp. 230ff; and Watchman Nee, *The Normal Christian Life* (Fort Washington, Penn.: Christian Literature Crusade, 1971). Watchman Nee's book offers a practical handbook for living amid the complex reality of the normal two-personality Christian psyche.

CHAPTER 6

1. Psalm 91:10 goes so far as to say that nothing which befalls a person of faith can possibly be evil! 2 Thessalonians 3:3 says flatly that God will keep the faithful person from evil. And Romans 8:28, putting the same truth a little differently, says that every event in the life of the faithful functions in collaboration with every other event to bring about the highest good.

CHAPTER 7

1. J. B. Watson, and R. Rayner, "Conditioned Emotional Reactions," *Journal of Experimental Psychology*, Vol. 3 (1920), pp. 1–14.

CHAPTER 8

1. Dietrich Bonhoeffer, tr. by B. H. Fuller, *The Cost of Discipleship* (New York: Macmillan, 1957). Pastor Bonhoeffer fulfilled this word literally when he was martyred by the Nazis in 1945 for his testimony to Christ.
2. Hebrews 10:32–36 urges endurance and joyful acceptance, which alone enable a Christian's faith to bring forth the *doing* of the will of God.
3. Rollo May, *The Meaning of Anxiety*, Revised Edition (New York: W. W. Norton, 1977).

CHAPTER 9

1. E. Jacobson, *Progressive Relaxation* (Chicago: University of Chicago Press, 1938), and *You Must Relax* (New York: McGraw-Hill, 1962).
2. The American Heart Association offers a variety of articles and resources related to physical activity at *www.americanheart.org*.
3. Paraphrase of Psalm 131:2.

4. Herbert Benson, M.D. *The Relaxation Response* (New York: William Marrow and Company, Inc., 1975).

CHAPTER 10

1. A number of psychological problems have anxiety at their base and have therefore been fruitfully treated with *exposure and response prevention*: phobias, for example, and certain kinds of obsessive-compulsive problems, anxieties about performance, and fears of other people.
2. R. L. Solomon and L. C. Wynne, "Traumatic Avoidance Learning: The Principles of Anxiety Conservation and Partial Irreversibility, *Psychology Review, 61*, (1954), pp. 353–385. See also R. L. Solomon, L. J. Kamin, and L. C. Wynne, "Traumatic Avoidance Learning: The Outcomes of Several Extinction Procedures With Dogs." *Journal of Abnormal Social Psychology, 48* (1953), pp. 291–302.
3. Some worriers aren't merely *worrying*, but *obsessing*. If you have recurring threatening thoughts that are obviously false but simply won't go away, they may be *obsessions*, and you may want to get professional help. Behavioral techniques and medications can be effective in helping obsessional thinking.
4. Summarized in *Prevention* magazine, March 1990, pp. 16–18.

CHAPTER 12

1. This is discussed in a remarkable passage, 1 John 5:4–5 (and following): "Everyone born of God overcomes the world. This is the victory that has overcome the world, even our faith. Who is it that overcomes the world? Only he who believes that Jesus is the Son of God."

CHAPTER 13

1. Check 1 Peter 1:22–2:3; 1 Thessalonians 2:13; John 17:20; Romans 10:17.
2. In, for example, the Classics Club edition, translated by B. Jowett, edited with introduction by Louise Ropes Loomis (Roslyn, New York: Walter J. Black, Inc., 1942).

CHAPTER 14

1. See Ephesians 6:10–17; 2 Timothy 4:7; Philippians 1:30; 1 Timothy 1:18.
2. David D. Burns, M.D., "How to Relax in a Crowd," condensed from Dr. Burns' books *The Feeling Good Handbook* and *Intimate Connections*, The Reader's Digest (January 1991), pp. 137–40.
3. Aaron T. Beck and Gary Emery, with Ruth L. Greenberg, *Anxiety Disorders and Phobias* (New York: Basic Books, Inc., 1985).
4. H. L. Weinberg, *Levels of Knowing and Existence* (Lakeville, Connecticut: Institute of General Semantics, 1973), p. 187. (Cited in Beck, Emery, and Greenberg, *ibid.*, p. 233).

CHAPTER 15

1. Dr. Wolpe believes that systematic desensitization works because of a process different from exposure that involves what learning psychologists call "extinction." Wolpe's theory holds that systematic desensitization is effective because of what he calls "reciprocal inhibition": that is, the pairing of anxiety-arousing scenes with a response which inhibits anxiety, thus conditioning these stimuli to a new, anxiety-inhibiting response. Readers interested in the issue can find Wolpe's discussion of it in *Life Without Fear*, Joseph Wolpe, M.D., with David Wolpe (Oakland, Calif.: New Harbinger Publications, 1988), pp. 120–21.

2. The method of exposing a person to the most anxiety-producing situation available, and deliberately eliciting strong anxiety until it diminishes is called "implosion." The method of exposing a person to life-situation anxiety elicitors is called "*in vivo*" desensitization. These are different techniques and are not necessarily always combined.

3. Albert Ellis, "Psychoneurosis and Anxiety Problems," in *Cognition and Emotional Disturbance*, Grieger, Russell & Grieger, Ingrid Zachary, eds. (New York: Human Sciences Press, Inc., 1982), p. 28.

CHAPTER 16

1. As in all the stories told in this book, the details are true, but in order to protect confidentiality, several histories have been blended together and identifying details altered.

2. Aaron T. Beck and Gary Emery, with Ruth L. Greenberg, *Anxiety Disorders and Phobias: A Cognitive Perspective* (New York: Basic Books, 1985).

3. I suppose, in order to preserve my reputation as a rather compulsive psychologist, I ought to note that in science the words "none" and "never" really should be replaced with phrases like "almost none" and "almost never." Theoretically, there is *some* probability, however tiny, of *anything* conceivable occurring somewhere sometime. But for practical purposes, these fears are groundless.

4. I'm not advising *everyone* to eliminate caffeine, just people whose anxiety threshold is so low every little bit helps. People who see themselves as living on the verge of panic like those described in this chapter should probably not drink coffee or other beverages containing caffeine. And of course no one should smoke.

5. *www.americanheart.org.*

CHAPTER 17

1. Here is a list of such promises. Look them up if you need strengthening in your belief that God promises to answer prayer: Isaiah 65:24; Psalm 10:17; Psalm 65:2; Matthew 7:7; Matthew 18:19–20; Matthew 21:22; Mark

11:22–26; John 14:13–14; John 15:7; John 16:23–24; Philippians 4:6; James 1:5–8; James 5:16; 1 John 3:22.

2. Norman P. Grubb, *Rees Howells: Intercessor* (Fort Washington, Penn.: The Christian Literature Crusade, 1975).

3. Here is a list of books detailing numerous remarkable accounts of prayer answered: *Remarkable Miracles*, G. C. Bevington (Plainfield, N.J.: Logos International, 1973); *Young Rebel in Bristol, Biography of George Mueller*, Faith Coxe Bailey (Chicago: Moody Press, 1958); *Realities: the Miracles of God Experienced Today*, M. Basilea Schlink, tr. by Larry Christenson and William Castell (Grand Rapids, Mich.: Zondervan Publishing House, 1966); *God's Smuggler*, Brother Andrew, with John and Elizabeth Sherrill (Old Tappan, N.J.: Fleming H. Revell, 1967); *Smith Wigglesworth: Apostle of Faith*, Stanley Howard Frodsham (Springfield, Mo.: Gospel Publishing House, 1972); *Kathryn Kuhlman*, Helen Kooiman Hosier (Old Tappan, N.J.: Fleming H. Revell, 1971); *Healing*, Father Francis MacNutt (New York: Bantam Books, Inc., 1977); *A Handbook of Holy Spirit Baptism*, Don Basham (Pittsburgh: Whitaker House, 1969); *Nine O'clock in the Morning*, Dennis J. Bennett (Plainfield, N.J.: Logos, 1970).

Many more such books could be added to the list. I have selected these at random from my own library.

4. For readers interested in experimental design, Dr. Byrd used a prospective, randomized, double-blind protocol with a treatment group of 192 subjects and a control group of 201 subjects. No differences were found between the groups at the beginning of treatment, but the treatment group had a significantly lower severity score during their hospital course ($p<.01$). Multivariant analysis separated the groups on the basis of the outcome variables ($p<.0001$). The control patients required ventilatory assistance, antibiotics, and diuretics more frequently than patients in the treatment group. Incidentally, since it was obviously not possible for Dr. Byrd to be certain that friends and relatives weren't praying for at least some of the patients in the control group, we might well assume the results are less spectacular than they would have been if members of the control group had absolutely no one praying for them.

5. See *The Door*, Mar-Apr 1990, pp. 17ff., for some excellent additional insights on the connection between contentment and happiness.

ABOUT THE AUTHOR

William Backus, Ph.D., founded the Center for Christian Psychological Services. Before his death in 2005, he was a licensed clinical psychologist and an ordained Lutheran clergyman. He wrote many books, including the bestselling *Telling Yourself the Truth* (coauthored with Marie Chapian).

Dr. William Backus

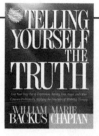

Change the Way You Think

Wrong thinking produces wrong emotions, reactions, and behavior—and unhappiness! Learning to deal with your thoughts is the first step on the road to healthy thinking and living. By identifying your own misbeliefs and replacing them with the truth, this book will help transform your life. Over half a million copies sold!

Telling Yourself the Truth by Dr. William Backus and Marie Chapian

Put the Book in Action

Based on the bestselling book *Telling Yourself the Truth*, this stand-alone workbook provides you with the tools you need to be free from the tyranny of anger, depression, anxiety, perfectionism, and other emotional difficulties. Through self-evaluation, growth exercises, and spiritual discipleship, you will identify your own misbeliefs and replace them with the truth, leading to a life of true happiness.

Learning to Tell Myself the Truth by Dr. William Backus